Statistics
for Biologists

Statistics
for Biologists

D. J. FINNEY, CBE, ScD, FRS, FRSE

Professor of Statistics,
University of Edinburgh
Director,
ARC Unit of Statistics

1980
LONDON AND NEW YORK
CHAPMAN AND HALL
150TH ANNIVERSARY

First published in 1980 by
Chapman and Hall Ltd
11 New Fetter Lane, London EC4P 4EE
Published in the USA by
Chapman and Hall
29 West 35th Street, New York NY 10001
Reprinted 1987

© 1980 D. J. Finney

ISBN 0 412 21540 3

Printed in Great Britain by
J. W. Arrowsmith Ltd., Bristol

British Library Cataloguing in Publication Data

Finney, David John
    Statistics for biologists—(Science paperbacks).
    1. Biometry
    I. Title II. Series
    519.5′02′4574   QH323.5

ISBN 0-412-21540-3

Contents

Sections marked* can be omitted at first reading.

Preface

This book has grown from nine hours of lectures, and about the same time in tutorial classes, that attempt to give first-year students of biology some understanding of statistics. I am convinced that such a short course should not be mathematical (though it can employ basic mathematical symbolism), and that it should give students an appreciation of statistical argument, even though this limits the amount of detailed instruction in techniques of analysis that can be included. A statistical cookery book would have been easier to write and much easier to read, but lacking in true educational content. I am more concerned to show 'why' than to present methods and rules. A further constraint, that of remaining within a reasonable price range, prevents reiteration of explanations: the reader is expected to remember what he has read, for he will not find standard terms and ideas explained afresh on each occasion of use.

Many books that introduce statistics to biologists blur distinctions and evade logical issues, for example by failing to emphasize the distinction between a parameter and an estimator from a sample or by neglecting the role of randomization. On this, I aim to be uncompromisingly correct – at least until reviewers point out my errors – but to do so through realistic examples rather than abstract symbolism. I insist that some mastery of symbols and exact terminology is as essential to biometric statistics as to any other exact discussion of science; I intend that the logic shall be absorbed by way of examples of biological problems without the formality of statement and proof that a mathematician would welcome.

One difficulty in constructing lectures or a book at this level is that most genuine data offer too many statistical problems simultaneously and often also involve biology that is unfamiliar to a first-year student. I have therefore adapted a problem of clinical medicine, chosen because no special scientific expertise is needed to understand it, and, by setting invented 'data' in two distinct contexts, have given myself a basis for questions and analyses that tie together a range of topics in the statistics of discrete and continuous variates and of experimental design. The text and the wide range of exercises refer to many problems of pure and applied biology in which statistical inference is essential – in genetics, ecology, seed testing, entomology, nutrition, agriculture, etc. Though full instruction in techniques must be sought elsewhere, methodological topics discussed include probability, χ^2 for contingency tables, the binomial. Normal and t-distributions, parameters and statistics, significance tests, paired and unpaired comparisons of means, standard errors of means, experimental design, randomization, sampling, regression, dose-response relations, calculators and computers. The book is designed for consecutive study, but sections marked with an asterisk can be omitted or postponed at a first reading. A teacher should increase its usefulness if he is prepared to add his own examples and experience to the structure that I adopt. A student who takes account of the structure, and who reads thoroughly, should find that he establishes a firm foundation of statistical understanding.

I am grateful to members of my own staff and to colleagues in other Departments whose comments on lecture notes have contributed to the organization of the book, to my secretarial staff who have patiently typed and checked a succession of versions, to my wife and daughter Katharine for help with the final text, and to three people whose suggestions to my publisher have led to many small improvements. I must also thank the editors of the *New Scientist* for permission to include Exercise 8.7.

D. J. FINNEY
Edinburgh
June 1979

1 Problems, data, questions

1.1 Introduction

The biological and social sciences used to be largely descriptive. They have become increasingly quantitative, with insistence that counting and measuring are essential to a proper understanding of the phenomena discussed. *Statistical science* is a discipline, and an ever-growing collection of methods, that aids the process of investigating quantitative problems in which inherent variability of material obscures simple relations. This is widely accepted in subjects as diverse as genetics, ecology, pharmacology and agriculture; in every field of pure or applied biology, however, to equip himself for his career a young scientist needs an appreciation of statistical ideas even if he is not prepared to become skilled in statistical practice. I write with special concern for any student of biology who developed a fear of mathematics when first introduced to quadratic equations, who struggled through school mathematics with ever-decreasing understanding, and who chose a biological science because he thought it non-mathematical. He will not read this book as easily as will a more mathematically able student, but he can understand almost everything important without dependence on other mathematical study. The aims and logic of mathematically-based statistical method can be appreciated with little mathematical skill. What is necessary is a willingness to think about problems with logical precision, and to read basic mathematical symbolism as part of the exact language of science.

Remember that quantitative problems include not only the obviously quantitative concerned with 'the number of', 'the weight of', etc.; some are more vaguely phrased and relate to 'more of', 'larger than', 'more variable than', etc. Progress with any such

1

problem requires that *data* are collected, 'analysed' in ways that can range from simple inspection to very complicated computation, and interpreted so as to throw light on aspects of the problem. As we shall see, to know numerical values is not enough. How data are collected is usually important to their interpretation; unless we ourselves have collected data according to a specified plan, we shall need to begin by asking many questions about their origin and nature. Note that I treat the word 'data' as plural, not just to be pedantic but in order to emphasize that data are many distinct entities that in combination give evidence on several aspects of a problem.

Mathematical symbols, conventional names for quantities (such as observations or the results of calculations) or for processes (such as 'divide', 'square this quantity'), are no more mysterious than any other class of technical names. You will not succeed in science unless you make yourself learn nomenclature and terminology that relates to various disciplines. You must distinguish H_2O from H_2O_2. You must recognize that the fact that H_2O rather than K_2O represents water is in one sense purely convention: the letter 'K' could have been consistently used to represent the first element in the periodic table. You must distinguish *Equus caballus* from *Escherichia coli*, but recognize that only an accident of language prevents the first from being a bacterium and the second a mammal. Similarly, to distinguish $(1 + x)^2$ from $(1 + x^2)$ and x from $\bar{x}$, or to recognize that y is conventionally a numerical value and Σ conventionally an order to add, is no more difficult and equally important. Chemists now rarely change the names and symbols for their elements, biologists are a little more prone to reclassify and rename, but mathematicians and statisticians are far from uniformity in the symbols they use. There are both reasons and excuses. I have tried to be self-consistent: I cannot conform to a standard usage, because different authors have different practices for many things that must have symbols. If you are ever to use any book on statistical method, you must be prepared to accept different conventions. The fact that I use 't' where some writers use 'd' or 'u' or 'z' has no more fundamental meaning, no more intellectual difficulty than the fact that some people say 'uomo' or 'mężczyzna' or 'hombre' or even 大 where you and I would say 'man'.

1.2 **Post-operative jaundice** (all information and data imaginary)

In order to link a number of ideas and methods, I shall refer repeatedly to one problem and set of data. I do not wish to restrict appreciation, and therefore I choose a problem easily understood by any reader with a scientific bent. Nor do I wish arithmetical complexity to obstruct the explanation of various procedures, and therefore I have invented numerically simple 'data'. My example originated in a medical question with which I was once concerned, but in order to avoid any misrepresentation I have invented a drug with imaginary properties.

The anaesthetic 'Gopain' is widely used for patients undergoing dental and other minor surgery. It is safe, easy to administer, and very effective in controlling pain. However, suspicions have arisen that, in consequence of receiving Gopain, some patients develop jaundice a few days later. At worst, this undesirable side-effect occurs in only a small proportion of patients, quite possibly the reported cases of jaundice developed independently of the anaesthetic, but the jaundice can be serious and even life-endangering. Current medical opinion is divided about whether the anaesthetic does or does not increase the risk of jaundice; we are participating in a study of the evidence. Medical experts suggest that, if Gopain increases the chances of jaundice, the jaundice is likely to occur sooner in patients who for any reason have had more than one recent exposure to Gopain. Table 1.1 contains records of 12 patients who developed jaundice after Gopain, 7 after their first surgery under this anaesthetic (Series D) and 5 after their second within 4 months (Series E). The table shows how soon jaundice occurred.

Table 1.1 Times to occurrence of jaundice in twelve surgical patients who received the anaesthetic Gopain (Times in days)

	Series D *First* *Gopain exposure*	*Series E* *Second* *Gopain exposure*
	14	4
	8	10
	3	7
	20	1
	18	8
	9	
	12	
Total	84	30
Mean	12	6

Data of appearance similar to these can arise in many different types of inquiry. For example, D and E might correspond to:

(i) Gains in weight of mice during 6 weeks on two different diets;
(ii) Heights of coconut seedlings at two different sites, 24 months after sowing;
(iii) Mercury content of cod caught in two different parts of the North Atlantic;
(iv) Times required by 7 untrained and 5 trained persons to perform a standard industrial task.

The units of measurement would differ, the numbers of individuals in D and E could differ, the methods of acquiring the data might be very different, but similar tables might be produced.

1.3 Questions relating to interpretation

A natural feature on which to concentrate attention is the simple average of the times, or in statistical terminology the *mean*, for each series. For E the mean is less than for D, but this is a statement only about the particular 12 patients. If the facts are to be of any use, we must extract from them more general information on the occurrence of jaundice after Gopain: we want an inference about the whole population or a definable segment of it. Two types of question need examination:

(a) Do the numerical values support the opinion that large numbers of records collected in the same way would continue to show a tendency for values in series E to be smaller than those in D?
(b) Do the individuals in D, E provide a fair and valid comparison of post-operative jaundice in patients who have had Gopain once or twice?

We shall be much more concerned with (a). Note that, despite an average difference of 6 days, D has one entry smaller than all except one of those in E. There is no clear separation of the two series. We must ask whether the difference is too great to be explained as due to chance.

Questions of type (b) are at least as important, but are more difficult to discuss without detailed knowledge of how the data were acquired. If the method of data collection is poor, whether unavoidably or from carelessness, the consequent biases may make conclusions under (a) irrelevant. For example, suppose that in a certain hospital all cases of post-operative jaundice occurring in 1977 or 1978 are collected; of the 58 records, 7 were after one exposure to Gopain and 5 after two. Even though D and E are comparable, we need to ask whether factors other than Gopain might be responsible for any difference between the means. Are patients who need frequent surgery more prone to early attacks of jaundice than those for whom surgery is a rare event, irrespective of the nature of the operation or the anaesthetic? Do the D tend to be young and healthy (e.g. accident cases), whereas E are debilitated by lengthy illness? Are cases at this hospital representative of the national population or only of a small region? For problems of this kind, cases are much too rare to be picked up in sufficient numbers at one hospital. If records from three hospitals are compounded, one must be alert to the possibility that the apparent effect is a consequence of differences between hospitals in the pattern of post-operative jaundice. Often records must come from information volunteered by physicians. New difficulties then arise: for example, cases thought unusual are more likely to be submitted than those conforming to what is regarded as standard.

These and like questions must be discussed thoroughly as part of the interpretative process for data of such inherent complexity. The major issue of whether or not Gopain sometimes *causes* jaundice is not under examination here; what is being studied is whether, if *jaundice occurs*, its time of appearance is affected by the number of exposures to Gopain. I shall return from time to time to matters concerning the nature of data and the design and planning of investigations. First I need to introduce you to numerical questions that lead to ideas on probability and on statistical tests.

1.4 An experiment

Table 1.1 relates to observations, but not to an *experiment*. The distinction is that in an experiment the investigator determines which treatment any individual shall receive, and does so in accordance with the logic of his research rather than to suit the needs of the subject. This places a severe restriction on experimentation on humans: patients received 1 or 2 Gopain exposures because of their medical needs, not just to provide scientific information. The logic of statistical inference is simpler and clearer for experiments than for observational data, and satisfactory discussion of cause and effect is now possible. Let us therefore suppose that we have results from the following carefully planned and conducted experiment:

'Twelve mice were divided arbitrarily into groups of 7 and 5, which then received single and double doses of Gopain, a drug fatal to mice. Table 1.1 shows the number of days for which each survived. (Alternatively, the entries in Table 1.1 could be measurements of any quality of the experimental animals 12 hours after treatment – concentration of a salt in the blood, area of inflammation at site of drug injection, weight of food consumed, etc.). Are the data consistent with a hypothesis that length of survival is independent of dosage?'

I shall later discuss the interpretation of Table 1.1 in this context as well as in relation to adverse reactions in humans. For an experiment, a division of the mice into two groups of 6 would be preferable, but unequal division is permissible. Unequal numbers are used here in order to illustrate more general procedures, and discussion of the ideal partition is deferred to Section 9.8.

1.5 More questions

When you are faced with numerical data that you need to interpret, whether you have collected them yourself or you have taken them from another source, begin by asking six questions:

1. WHAT are the data? What size of numbers, and to what accuracy of measurement and recording?

2. WHAT are the units? Inches, miles, cm, cm^2, $g\ cm^{-2}$, etc.?

3. ARE the values reasonable? If the data are annual rainfalls, are they sensible in relation to what is known of the locality? If they are human weights in kg, does the occurrence of 10.5 or 418.2 cast any doubts on trustworthiness?

4. HOW were they measured? Dangers of bias may be inherent in the measuring instrument, in the manner of its use, or in the recording. Thus a stop-watch might be running fast, the user may tend to

5. HOW were they acquired?

6. WHAT logical structures are present?

start it late relative to a phenomenon he is measuring, the user may round downwards all fractions of a minute. For the Gopain records, does 'days' mean 'to the nearest day' or completed days at 10.00 each morning? Was reliability of recording altered at week-ends?

How were the individual persons, animals, plants, cells, transistors, cans of oil, etc., chosen for measurement from all those available? Were there any features of the process of choice that would limit, or tend to bias, inferences from the data? If recording the consequences of Gopain had stopped after 10 days, series D would have consisted only of the 3 values 8, 3, 9 with a mean of 6.7 to compare with 6.0 for series E.

Does each value recorded refer to an independent animal, or were some animals recorded more than once? Were all animals unrelated, were some litter mates, or were there other family relations? Did some share the same environment because they were caged together?

If you neglect these questions, you may end with statistical analyses that look exactly like text-book examples but that are in reality nonsense – perhaps silly nonsense with absurd conclusions that make you distrust statistics when the fault is your own, perhaps dangerous nonsense because conclusions look plausible yet rest on false assumptions.

EXERCISES

1.1 The arm spans of the 150 adult male employees of a certain organization were measured. These were (recorded to the nearest cm)

173√	186√	180√	170√	186√	179√
193√	172√	187√	159√	194√	188√
178√	171√	184√	174√	181√	179√
186√	178√	165√	163√	184√	179√
178√	186√	176√	173√	174√	182√
180√	190√	180√	179√	164√	165√
170√	166√	181√	174√	170√	171√
180√	171√	177√	179√	169√	180√
171√	181√	178√	170√	179√	175√
177√	179√	162√	173√	180√	185√
173√	166√	168√	161√	169√	167√
184√	188√	179√	175√	180√	169√
181√	188√	173√	164√	176√	172√
177√	174√	183√	188√	191√	172√
168√	168√	169√	183√	174√	156√
167√	180√	183√	182√	180√	177√
167√	180√	172√	165√	184√	190√
183√	185√	186√	169√	188√	173√
173√	169√	167√	156√	173√	170√
184√	184√	173√	180√	182√	166√
182√	178√	163√	171√	176√	192√
165√	164√	178√	170√	167√	187√
169√	183√	183√	172√	174√	183√
177√	170√	171√	173√	174√	173√
167√	179√	184√	185√	182√	188√

(The '√' marks indicate that, in my original working, I checked the copying of each entry, starting from the last and working backward. Anyone copying data, however great his experience, needs this kind of precaution.) Prepare a summary table that shows how many lie in each of the classes 156, 157, ..., 194. Do not attempt to count each group directly. The simple and safe method is: write on consecutive lines each of the possible values, read through the table and make a tally mark for each entry on its summary line, and finally count the tally marks on each line.

1.2 By the nature of the recording, 173 means 'the span exceeded 172.5 and did not exceed 173.5'. Now combine pairs of groups from Exercise 1.1 so as to have frequencies of men in classes 156–157, 158–159, ..., 194–195. Note that the midpoints of the classes are 156.5 (for all between 155.5 and 157.5), 158.5, etc. Also combine successive sets of 3 groups, so as to give frequencies in classes 156–158, 159–161, etc., successive sets of 5 (156–160, 161–165, etc.) and successive sets of 10 (156–165, 166–175, 176–185, 186–195). Comment on why neither the frequency tabulation in Exercise 1.1 nor that last mentioned are very satisfactory as summaries of data.

1.3 Draw *histograms* or block diagrams for each of the groupings in Exercises 1.1 and 1.2. If you do not understand these terms, refer to the solution on page 135; note particularly the positioning of the blocks on the horizontal axis and the fact that each histogram has the same *total* area, scaled to correspond to the 150 observations.

1.4 (Unless you have some intuitive ideas about probability, do not attempt the second part.)

A coin is spun 4 times. List all the possible sequences of heads and tails that can occur. How many are there? How many of these have:

  (i) an equal number of heads and tails?
  (ii) more heads than tails?
  (iii) more tails than heads?
  (iv) no. of heads − no. of tails = 1?
  (v) no. of heads − no. of tails = 2?

On the assumption that the coin is unbiased, write down the probability for each of these five possibilities. The experiment is repeated with a new 'coin' that is strongly biased in favour of heads. State, qualitatively only, what kind of change would occur for the probability in (ii), (iii) and (iv).

1.5 (This question is to encourage you to think about probability *before* you read Chapter 3; do not worry if you find it beyond you at present.)

You are likely to have some intuitive ideas on probability. Can you see the error in the following, and give the correct answer?

'What is the probability that heads will turn up at least once in two spins of a fair coin? Answer: Only three different events are possible:

  (i) heads the first time, making a second spin unnecessary;
  (ii) tails the first time, heads the second;
  (iii) tails both times.

Two of the three cases are favourable, and therefore the required probability is 2/3'.

1.6 Tablets containing the medicinal drug Clioquinol used to be widely used as a remedy for minor stomach disorders; they did not require to be prescribed by a doctor. Unfortunately, various unpleasant side effects (some fatal) were reported, primarily from Japan. An enquiry was made from a sample of Japanese immigrants in another country. Each was asked whether he or she had taken Clioquinol at any time during the previous five years and, if the answer was 'yes', at what rate per day. An average dose per day, calculated as the mean of the doses stated (including zero for each respondent who did not take Clioquinol during the five years), was used to indicate the total annual consumption of the drug in the Japanese community. Comment critically on the collection of information and on this mean dose.

2 Probability and other definitions

As in any scientific activity, statistical science requires careful use of some technical terms. I shall endeavour to keep these to a minimum, but must introduce a few before I explain probability.

2.1 Population

Every set of statistical data must be interpreted in relation to the population from which it comes. In our usage, a population is any actual or conceptual collection of individual items, defined by stated characteristics. For example:

(i) All university students in Boston in 1980;
(ii) All university students within the city of Boston, Massachusetts at noon on 1 December 1980;
(iii) All deciduous trees in the Black Forest;
(iv) All coins in my pocket;
(v) All coins that at any time in my life are in my pocket;
(vi) All progeny of a particular rat;
(vii) All bacteria in a specific bottle of milk;
(viii) All persons who undergo surgery in Scotland in 1980;
(ix) All those in (viii) who received Gopain before the surgery;
(x) All those in (viii) who developed jaundice during the 4 weeks after surgery;
(xi) All persons common to (ix) and (x);
(xii) All flights from London Airport in November 1980 that left more than 5 minutes late.

A population may require very exact definition in order to make it logically and operationally adequate. Note that (ii) above is more

11

exact than (i): it avoids any doubt about which Boston is intended and removes vagueness about the meaning of 'in', but the term 'university student' is imprecise. Points of this kind assume great importance in international statistical comparisons. You should examine each of (iii) to (xii) and consider how the definitions need to be tightened. What is the boundary of the Black Forest? What is a tree? (This raises questions of species and of the stage at which a small seedling is classed as a tree.) How are trees close to the boundary to be classified? Is an antique or a counterfeit coin to be included? Is attention restricted to live rats? How do we take account of changes in a bacterial population while we are working with it? What is surgery? How do we classify a flight that leaves on time but returns after 10 minutes because of a fault? Such queries, which may be vital to conclusions, can be answered fully only from knowledge of the subject of study.

A population may be *finite* (coins in my pocket, persons who began a trans-Atlantic flight today) or *infinite* (all circles that could be placed on this page without crossing the edges, all areas of 1 ha that could be demarcated within a forest). Many finite populations are so large that for practical purposes they can be regarded as infinite (all leaves on a large tree, all motor vehicles currently registered in the UK). Most populations that concern us consist of real objects; some (especially the infinite) are purely conceptual or hypothetical.

2.2 Variate

A *variate* is any property of an individual (person, tree, rat, flight) that can be expressed in numerical terms. We are interested in the values of a variate (sometimes of several distinct variates) that relate to the different members of a population. A variate may be readily measured or determined for any member of the population, it may be the product of a complicated analysis or laborious counting, it may be unobtainable without destroying the member of the population. For example:

   (i) The height of a 12-year old boy;

  (ii) The percentage calcium in the blood of the same boy;

 (iii) The number of leaves on a tree;

 (iv) The liver weight of a rat (obtainable only by killing the rat);

  (v) The number of days between surgery and recognition of jaundice in population (x) of Section 2.1;

(vi) The length of delay in departure of a plane;
(vii) The number of heads obtained in 1 spin of a coin (a way of expressing a dichotomous classification by a variate that can take only the value 0, 1);
(viii) The sex of a rat (arbitrarily denoted by 0 or 1).

Again exact definition is needed: When shall the boy be measured? What is the instant of plane departure?

A variate may be *discrete* (usually something that is counted in whole numbers, such as the number of completed days, the number of leaves, the number of female patients, or other distinct categories), or *continuous* (measured on a continuous scale, as for a weight, a density, a time or an electrical resistance). Avoid the careless and sloppy phrasing of a 'continuous population' or a 'discrete population', even though this seems unambiguous when only one variate is under consideration. If we are discussing for each plane its delay time and the number of passengers, we must distinguish between the population, the continuous variate (time), and the discrete variate (passengers).

Some variates, by virtue of their definitions, have finite ranges (the number of females in a litter of 8 mice cannot be less than 0 or greater than 8, the percentage calcium in the blood cannot be less than 0 or more than 100). Others have infinite ranges, meaning that there is no limit that cannot be exceeded (the number of mice that must be reared before 12 females are obtained, the number of minutes a plane is delayed). For many variates with finite ranges, the limit is indeterminate: no one smokes 2000 cigarettes in a day, but we cannot determine a limit in such a way as to say 178 is possible and 179 is impossible

2.3 Sample

Often a scientist is interested in the behaviour of a variate throughout a population, but measurement of every member of the population is impracticable. One cannot envisage catching and weighing every rabbit in a study area or measuring the length of every leaf on a tree. Not infrequently, the restriction is stronger than a consideration of economy or speed. The measurement may involve destruction of the individual (weight of rabbit's heart or chemical constitution of a leaf), so that full records for a population would prevent any continuing study of that population. A *sample* of a population is some segment of the population that is examined and measured as an aid to investigating properties of the parent population. As a sample of university students or of young adults, I might take all members of a first-year zoology class in one university. I might pour 2 ml from a bottle of milk as a sample for bacteriological study. I might record flight delays only on 2 days per week. Thus I measure the variate on the members of a sample, and then become involved in inference from sample to population.

2.4   Representativeness and randomness

Though any part of a population can be regarded as a sample, for the sample to be useful in making inferences about the population it clearly must in some sense be representative. In some respects, first-year zoology students might prove representative at least of the student body of their own university – in height and weight, for example, but not in age or in knowledge of modern history. Why? Possibly, indeed, biologists and arts students differ in average height. My 2 ml sample of milk will not have a representative bacterial population unless I ensure that the bottle is well-mixed before pouring. I suspect that traffic congestion increases flight delays on some days of the week, and that to sample Fridays and Saturdays only would give a misleading picture. If the 150 men in Exercise 1.1 were lined up in decreasing order of height before their arm spans were measured, the first 10 measurements would be a poor sample of the whole. Because of a tendency for tall men to have long arms, the 10 tallest might all have spans in excess of 185 cm. In a more complex manner, this is part of the trouble with the Gopain data in Chapter 1. Physicians reported voluntarily, and therefore possibly the records are biased towards serious or striking cases, or towards hospitals already alerted to a special interest in the problem.

The only safe way of ensuring that a sample is representative is to introduce an element of *randomness* into its selection. After the population has been exactly defined, the sample is drawn by lot. Thus to select a sample of 200 students one could identify every registered student by a number and select 200 by an actual lottery. For the trees in the Black Forest, one might mark on a map small randomly situated areas, say 50 m square, and use all trees within these. For the flights from the airport, one might choose random times on each day, and then record the first delayed flight after, say 11.43 a.m. on 4 November. A better procedure would be to choose random hours during the day and to record the delay for every flight scheduled to depart in each 60-minute period; some times of day may be excessively liable to delays. Special 'tables of random numbers' are widely used by statisticians and other scientists to make choice entirely arbitrary and objective, and to ensure that each unit in the population has the same chance of inclusion in the sample.

2.5 Means and related properties

You will be familiar with the notion of the *mean* (the arithmetic mean or simple average) of a set of observations. This, the most widely useful single quantity for characterizing observations, is found by adding all values of the variate and dividing by their number. In Exercise 1.1 the total of 150 arm spans is 26 418 cm; the mean arm span (in cm) is

$$26\,418/150 = 176.12.$$

We must distinguish between the *population mean* and the *sample mean* for a specified sample. For an infinite population, in order to define the population mean we must invoke ideas of limits as larger and larger samples are taken; the formal mathematics is troublesome, but the general concept of a mean of all decimals between 0.5 and 0.6 or a mean area of all oak leaves is not difficult.

You should be aware of two other quantities, distinct from the mean, that also tell something about the location or position of the variate in a sample. The *median* is the middle value when the observations are arranged in order from smallest to largest. In a sample of 139 arm spans, the median would be the 70th (from either end) when they are ranked in order. In a sample of 150, we conventionally define the median to be halfway between the 75th and the 76th; for the arm spans, the 75th and the 76th are both 177 cm, which is therefore also the median. The *mode* is the most commonly occurring value. It is of limited utility for a continuous variate in a sample (three spans recorded as 173 cm may really be 173.41, 172.68 and 173.08), but is sometimes useful with a discrete variate: the modal number of children per family might be 2, even though the mean was 3.16. The arm spans in Exercise 1.1 have two modes, 173 cm and 180 cm each occurring 11 times. Median and mode can also be defined for populations, but I shall not explain details here.

2.6 Parameters and statistics

A *parameter* is any numerical property of a population. The population mean, median, and mode are known as *parameters of location* – they relate to the general location of numerical values of the variate. For example, each of them could be used to indicate how lateness of flight departures in November compared with lateness in July. They will not necessarily give the same qualitative impression: the median might be greater in July than in November, yet the mean greater in November than in July. For variates of similar character, however, these three parameters will often behave similarly. Marked anomalies should arouse suspicion of errors in arithmetic or features of a population that call for special comment. Note that a variate can have two or more modes, for example if the population is not homogeneous but perhaps includes individuals from several different species in which the variate takes very different values (a size measurement on the population of waterfowl on a lake might show a mode for geese, a mode for ducks, and a mode for some smaller species).

A *statistic* is any numerical property calculated for a sample. Often a correspondence exists between sample statistics and population parameters, and inferences about an unknown parameter may be based on calculations with the known sample statistic. In particular, we can find mean, median, and mode of a sample as *statistics of location*. Do not assume that there is always a good correspondence: sometimes a parameter is best estimated by a sample statistic that looks very different in form. Suppose for a moment that the data in Exercise 1.1 related to the whole population of men in a small community. The maximum span is 194 cm, a parameter of the population. In a random sample of 8 men, the largest span cannot exceed 194 cm and may by chance be substantially less (perhaps only 175 cm). A population maximum is rarely well estimated by the maximum of a sample, and indeed satisfactory estimation of a population maximum is difficult. Some sample statistics have rather different purposes and do not correspond directly to parameters. Other parameters and statistics of location exist but I have mentioned the three most important. When in doubt, use the mean, but remember that it may sometimes fail to show the behaviour of a variate adequately.

2.7 Probability

Most people have intuitive ideas of probability, or at least use the word 'probable' in general conversation: 'Snowfall is more probable on 1 January than on 1 April', 'Jaundice is more probable within 10 days of surgery for patients who have had Gopain than for those who have had another anaesthetic'. We need to express our ideas quantitatively, so as to be able to assign a numerical value to probability. Some statisticians have sought to base a formal system of probability theory on personal beliefs and subjective judgement. In this sense, one can speak of the probability that there is a 'monster' in Loch Ness, or the probability that your favourite football team will win next Saturday. Such a system can be made internally consistent, and may be a valuable aid to quantitative assessment of whether or not to embark on a certain action, for example to change employment, to build a new factory, to lay a bet or to start a new experiment. The decisions involve personal judgement, not only of the benefits that will accrue from alternative outcomes but also of the numerical magnitudes assigned to any relevant probabilities.

This approach is seldom appropriate to scientific inference, where the emphasis is usually on adding to knowledge of the world rather than on taking decisions. Given the same information, different reasonable and intelligent people can disagree totally on the numerical value that expresses a personal belief – a belief that at least 1 cm of rain will fall tomorrow, that the next patient to receive Gopain will develop jaundice, or that a particular rat carries a recessive gene for blindness. The preferred approach to probability is by way of relative frequency, which achieves quantification objectively but needs some appreciation of a mathematical limit. Consider records of any repeated observation or trial that must have one of two outcomes:

spin of a coin   – outcome Heads or Tails,
birth of a child   – outcome Male or Female,
sowing of a seed   – outcome Germination or not,
treatment of a patient – outcome Cure or Failure.

Suppose the coin to be spun very many times, or births to be recorded in a hospital over a long period, or a large number of seeds to be sown and the sequence of germination records studied. Table 2.1 illustrates what might be found.

For a good coin, or for the sex of a child, the proportion would be nearer to 0.50, but the same sort of pattern would emerge: the relative frequency of one outcome oscillates irregularly but slowly stabilizes and the oscillations become steadily less in amplitude. If you doubt this, experiment for yourself by recording, say, 200 spins of a coin and noting the proportion of heads after every 10 spins.

Table 2.1 Summarized records of a sequence of records of seed germination, to illustrate approach of proportion germinating to the limit 'probability'

Numbers of seed Recorded	Germinated	Proportion, or relative frequency
10	10	1.00
20	17	0.85
30	26	0.87
50	46	0.92
100	95	0.95
200	186	0.930
500	479	0.958
1 000	949	0.949
5 000	4 792	0.958 4
10 000	9 543	0.954 3
50 000	47 781	0.955 62
⋮	⋮	⋮

and so on

Limit = ??

We define the probability of a particular outcome to be the limit to which the relative frequency tends as the number of trials increases indefinitely. We can never determine it exactly by experiment, but we can believe in its existence and approximate closely if we make enough trials – for the seed germination perhaps a number such as 0.954 807 1 . . . . We should then have also the complementary probability that a seed fails to germinate, 0.045 192 8 . . . . We could form similar but more elaborate records if there were more than two possible outcomes. Thus for

seed germinates and is correct species,
seed germinates and is wrong species,
seed germinates and is unidentifiable species,
seed fails to germinate.

or

treated patient recovers full health,
treated patient remains disabled,
treated patient dies,

each outcome has its probability. Exact definition of the words in each phrase is essential if the probability is to have unique meaning.

From consideration of relative frequencies, it is evident that the probability of occurrence of A as the outcome of an observation, denoted by $Pr(A)$, possesses certain properties:

(1) $0 \leqslant Pr(A) \leqslant 1$
(2) $Pr(A) = 0$ means that A can *never* happen ('exposed face of coin shows Queen's head and value');
(3) $Pr(A) = 1$ means that A must always happen ('exposed face of coin contains letter E');
(4) If A, B, C, D, ... account for all possible outcomes and no outcome is included under two different heads (see Section 3.1),

$$Pr(A) + Pr(B) + Pr(C) + Pr(D) + \ldots = 1; \qquad [2.1]*$$

e.g.

$$Pr(\text{germination}) + Pr(\text{non-germination}) = 1,$$

$$Pr(\text{cure}) + Pr(\text{disabled}) + Pr(\text{death}) = 1,$$

or, for the number of live aphids on a rose bush,

$$Pr(0) + Pr(1) + Pr(2) + \ldots = 1,$$

where the relation must be true even though we are not prepared to state an upper limit. In this last example, we might overcome the awkwardness of the large number of classes and the uncertain upper limit by grouping, writing perhaps

$$Pr(0) + Pr(1 \text{ to } 10) + Pr(11 \text{ to } 25) + Pr(26 \text{ to } 100) + \ldots$$
$$+ Pr(\text{over } 5000) = 1$$

where the last class is open-ended but 5000 has been chosen as sufficiently great to make 'over 5000' a rather rare class.

EXERCISES

2.1 Means of the thirty groups of 5 spans in Exercise 1.1 have been calculated and arranged in the same pattern as the full table. Verify the first of these and find the 4 that are omitted:

181.6	178.6	178.4	167.8	183.8	181.4
175.6	177.4	175.6	175.0	172.4	175.2
176.6	176.8	174.4	174.2	178.0	167.2
174.8	179.6	176.2	?	?	175.2
172.0	174.8	175.8	?	?	184.6

* All formulae numbered in [ ] should be remembered.

Find how many of these lie in the groups of width 5.0 cm used in Exercise 1.2 (165.5–170.5, 170.5–175.5, ...) and compare with the histogram in Exercise 1.3.

2.2 Suppose span has been recorded for 5000 men. You might prepare histograms for (i) the individuals, (ii) 1000 means of 5, (iii) 500 means of 10, (iv) 200 means of 25, (v) 100 means of 50. How would you expect these to appear relative to one another? What light does this throw on why a biologist chooses to use a mean of several individuals (e.g. weights of mice, lengths of plant stems, sizes of bacterial colonies) rather than single values?

2.3 What practical problems might you encounter in taking random samples of 100 from the following populations:

    (i) All members of a professional society;
    (ii) All your red blood cells;
    (iii) All seeds in a bag containing perhaps 50 000 of the size of pinheads;
    (iv) All users of a large reference library?

Consider carefully any dangers of bias in taking as samples the first 100 members to arrive at the society's annual conference, 100 red cells from a small volume withdrawn from you by a doctor, 100 seeds counted from the contents of a spoon inserted into the bag, the first person to enter the library after 9.00, 10.00, 11.00, ... next Monday, until 100 different users have been obtained.

2.4 The Faculty of Science in the University of Z contains 600 men and 400 women students. Of the men, 15% this year attend at least one course in mathematics, and of the women 10%. Find

    (i) The proportion of *all* students who attend at least one mathematics course;
    (ii) The proportion of women among students who attend at least one mathematics course.

(Compare with Exercise 3.3)

3 Combining probabilities

3.1 Mutual exclusion and independence

The word *event* is used as a general term for one of the possible outcomes from a *trial* or observational situation. Section 2.7 discusses several trials with outcomes that must be one of two events (spin of a coin, birth of a child, etc.), and later refers to trials with outcomes that can be classified as one of three or more events.

Alternative events are said to be *mutually exclusive* if it is logically impossible for two of them to occur simultaneously, or to be simultaneously correct descriptions of the outcome of the trial. The two examples near the end of Section 2.7 were of this kind; if a patient remains disabled he cannot have recovered full health or died. On the other hand, four events such as

patient recovers full health,
patient remains disabled,
patient returns to employment,
patient never returns to previous residence,

are not mutually exclusive; the third and fourth do not exclude one another or either of the first two.

Two trials are said to be *independent* if knowledge of the outcome of either does not affect the probabilities of possible outcomes of the other. Whereas mutual exclusion is primarily a matter of exact phraseology and simple logic, independence is difficult to secure absolutely and is indeed perhaps more an empirical truth than a logical. This reflects the fact that among natural phenomena interdependence is the usual state; most things interact with one another and although the effects of this may often be small, total independence is rare. In order to illustrate events for which independence can scarcely be doubted, I have been obliged to choose extreme instances of little intrinsic interest, but careful study of them should make clear the meaning of independence. Consider two 'trials' or observations, for each of which the outcome must be one of two mutually exclusive events. Each involves a simple dichotomous (two-way) classification:

   (1) A child under 14 years old, chosen at random from all those resident in your street is more than 150 cm tall *or* is not so tall,

   (2) a coin taken at random from your pocket is dated 1976 or later *or* it bears an earlier date.

These are totally unconnected; neither can influence the other, nor can the two results have any common cause; they must be statistically independent. A further observation might relate to one of the alternative events:

   (3) the child chosen in (1) is less than 5 years of age *or* is older; the category found here is certainly not independent of the outcome of (1), although it also is independent of (2). Consider also

   (4) the child chosen in (1) weighs less than 55 kg *or* weighs at least 55 kg,

   (5) the child chosen in (1) drinks at least 1 litre of milk per day *or* less than 1 litre.

Evidently the classifications represented by observations (4) and (1) are non-independent, for a heavy child has a greater probability of also being tall than does a light child. The non-independence of (4) and (3) is even more obvious: if a child weighs 55 kg, the probability of being under 5 years old is practically zero. The status of (5) is less obvious, but a large daily consumption of milk is presumably more common among young and small children than among older ones and to *assume* (5) independent of (1), (3), or (4) would be rash. Note that the reference population is relevant. In Section 2.7 if we restrict all discussions to seeds from one parent plant, four such seeds randomly chosen and tested for germination under standard conditions will provide four independent observations in respect of that parent. Similarly, if the population is defined as all seeds from a plot of many plants, germination records from four (or 400) randomly selected seeds will provide independent evidence on the probability of germination in the population; now, however, four seeds from *one* plant do not give independent evidence on the population since they may have a common inheritance of good (or of poor) germination.

3.2 **Addition of probabilities**

If A and B are two mutually exclusive events (which may be either the only possible alternatives such as 'heads' and 'tails' or may be two from a larger set), for example

A: patient died,
B: patient survived but was disabled,

(where 'survival and complete recovery' is a third possibility), then very obviously

no. of persons who are (A or B) = no. who are A + no. who are B.

The derivation of probability from relative frequency shows that

$$Pr(A \text{ or } B) = Pr(A) + Pr(B).$$

A scientist is often concerned with categories that are not mutually exclusive; for example, a third event might be

C: patient survived and resumed previous employment.

Now A and C are obviously mutually exclusive, but B and C may 'overlap' and precautions are needed in order to avoid double counting. By linguistic convention, the word 'or' is to be understood as meaning 'either or both', so that 'B or C' must be interpreted as 'at least one of B and C is true and possibly both'. With full generality, we can write

no. who are (B or C) = no. who are B + no. who are C
$$\qquad\qquad - \text{no. who are both B and C};$$

the third term on the right takes account of the fact that patients with both characteristics are included in the first term on the right and again in the second. Division by the total number of patients leads to the general addition rule for probabilities:

$$Pr(B \text{ or } C) = Pr(B) + Pr(C) - Pr(BC), \qquad [3.1]$$

where 'BC' is a shorthand symbol for 'both B and C' (patients who resume employment despite disability).

3.3 **Multiplication of probabilities**

We frequently want to discuss the occurrence of compound events consisting of the occurrence of two or more simple events in separate trials. If two events have independent probabilities, the probability that both occur is the product of the separate probabilities. For example, suppose that we have seeds with probability 0.96 of germination and a well-balanced coin, and we put a sequence of coin results alongside seed records so as to have

$$+ H, + T, + T, + H, - T, + H, + T, + H, - H, \ldots,$$

where $+$ represents germination, H represents heads. Then

$$Pr(\text{seed germinates and coin shows H}) = 0.96 \times 0.5 = 0.48,$$
$$Pr(\text{seed fails and coin shows H}) = 0.04 \times 0.5 = 0.02,$$

and so on. From consideration of relative frequencies, a fraction 0.96 of seeds will germinate, and independence ensures that half of these will be associated with H.

We are unlikely to be interested in such an odd combination of events, but results on independent testing of several seeds are more useful. If four seeds are independently tested,

$$Pr(\text{nos. 1, 4 germinate and nos. 2, 3 fail}) = 0.96 \times 0.04 \times 0.04 \times 0.96,$$
$$Pr(\text{nos. 1, 3 germinate and nos. 2, 4 fail}) = 0.96 \times 0.04 \times 0.96 \times 0.04,$$

not surprisingly the same value for both. Similarly

$$Pr(\text{all fail}) = (0.04)^4,$$
$$Pr(\text{80 seeds independently tested all germinate}) = (0.96)^{80}.$$

Note that independence is essential. With a fair coin,

$$Pr(\text{coin shows H } and \text{ date is upwards}) \neq 0.5 \times 0.5.$$

For recent British coins, this probability is 0.5 and for older coins it is 0; look at some coins to see why this is so. Again, suppose that in some large population of men

$$Pr(\text{span} \geqslant 182\,\text{cm}) = 0.2$$

and

$$Pr(\text{height} < 170\,\text{cm}) = 0.3.$$

Then we cannot reasonably state:

$$Pr(\text{span} \geqslant 182\,\text{cm and height} < 170\,\text{cm}) = 0.2 \times 0.3 = 0.06.$$

Think in terms of relative frequencies! Though some short men may have long arms, more commonly short men will have spans less than average. If we measured a sample of 1000 men, we would be surprised to find

		Height (cm)		
		< 170	≥ 170	Total
Span (cm)	< 182	224	566	790
	≥ 182	56	154	210
	Total	280	720	1000

even though the proportions in the margins of the table (0.21 large span, 0.28 small stature) are close to the population values. The feature that should strike us as odd is that the proportion of large spans is almost the same for short men as for tall. A much more natural state of affairs would be

		Height (cm)		
		< 170	≥ 170	Total
Span (cm)	< 182	264	526	790
	≥ 182	16	194	210
	Total	280	720	1000

Here the proportion of long arms among the tall men is much higher than among the short (a proportion 194/720 or 0.269, as against 0.057).

3.4 Conditional probabilities

In a sense all probabilities are conditional: the statement that $Pr(\text{span} \geq 182\,\text{cm}) = 0.2$ was conditional on the choice of a man from a specific population (it excluded children, gorillas, chairs, and many other possessors of arms), but the condition was clear from the start and did not need to be made explicit in the $Pr(. . .)$. Generalization of the simple rule of multiplying probabilities requires explicit recognition of relevant conditions. The last table in Section 3.3 might arise in a sample from a population in which

$$Pr(\text{span} \geq 182\,\text{cm}|\text{height} < 170\,\text{cm}) = 0.05$$
$$Pr(\text{span} \geq 182\,\text{cm}|\text{height} \geq 170\,\text{cm}) = 0.3,$$

where the symbol | introduces the condition. This notation illustrates what I said in Section 1.1 about the need to comprehend symbolism even though operating with it may be more complicated mathematically than you can follow. Thus the first of these two statements is a condensed way of saying 'The probability that a member of the sample whose height is less than 170 cm has a span of 182 cm or more equals 0.05.' Many words and much confusion are saved by adopting a standardized notation. Of course these numerical probabilities are mentioned here only for illustration, and many other values would agree satisfactorily with the sample records (e.g. 0.04 and 0.27; see Section 4.3).

Suppose that A, B represent two distinct events relating to members of a population, such as

A: span $\geqslant 182$ cm

B: height < 170 cm

or, in an analysis of hospital records,

A: a record refers to a female patient

B: a record refers to a blood-tested patient.

Hence once more we have two out of many categories into which patients might be placed, and some patients will be in both A and B. If N is the total number of patients in the records, it is self evident that

$$\frac{\text{no. who are both A and B}}{N} = \frac{\text{no. who are A}}{N}$$
$$\times \frac{\text{no. who are both}}{\text{no. who are A}}$$

(since 'no. who are A' can be cancelled in the two fractions on the right). Taking the limiting values of these relative frequencies, we obtain

Pr(A and B both true) $= Pr$(A is true) $\cdot Pr$(B is true|A is true)

and similarly

Pr(A and B both true) $= Pr$(B is true) $\cdot Pr$(A is true|B is true).

This is often abbreviated to

$$Pr(AB) = Pr(A) \cdot Pr(B|A) = Pr(B) \cdot Pr(A|B). \qquad [3.II]$$

Only if

$$Pr(B|A) = Pr(B)$$

is the event B statistically independent of A; it then follows that

$$Pr(A|B) = Pr(A),$$

and the simple result

$$Pr(AB) = Pr(A) \cdot Pr(B)$$

is true. You must regard the general formula, Equation [3.II], as the basic equation, unless and until you are sure of independence. In practice, perfect independence is not common. Are we certain that men born in a leap year are not on average larger (or smaller) than those born in other years? Only if we are do we have the independence condition:

$$Pr(\text{span} \geqslant 182\,\text{cm}|\text{born in a leap year}) = Pr(\text{span} \geqslant 182\,\text{cm}).$$

3.5 Finite populations

A word on finite populations may be helpful, because for them probabilities and relative frequencies can coincide. Suppose that we have a population of 5 mice, 3 white named W_1, W_2, W_3 and 2 brown named B_1, B_2. If one is chosen at random, rather obviously

$$Pr(\text{white}) = 3/5.$$

Similarly, if 2 mice are chosen simultaneously, the 10 possibilities are

$$W_1 W_2,\ W_1 W_3,\ W_1 B_1,\ W_1 B_2,\ W_2 W_3,\ W_2 B_1,\ W_2 B_2,\ W_3 B_1,\ W_3 B_2,$$
$$B_1 B_2$$

and all are equally likely. Therefore

$$Pr(2\ \text{white}) = 3/10,$$
$$Pr(1\ \text{of each}) = 6/10,$$
$$Pr(2\ \text{brown}) = 1/10.$$

The concept of a limit of relative frequency is still relevant. Although we have only 5 mice, we can also talk about an infinite population of repeated trials of 'select 2 at random from the 5'; if this were tried, the relative frequency of 2 white would oscillate around 3/10 and approach this as a limit.

3.6 Expectation

We frequently need, as a basis for comparisons, the numbers that would occur in different classes if observed frequencies conformed exactly to probabilities. For example, in the tables at the end of Section 3.3, if $Pr(A) = 0.2$ and $Pr(B) = 0.3$ were *known* to be the probabilities for large span and small stature respectively, we can calculate *expected numbers* or *expectations* on the hypothesis of independence. One such is

$$1000 \times 0.2 \times 0.3 = 60$$

for short, long-armed individuals. Thus we obtain the table

| | | Height (cm) | | |
		< 170	≥ 170	Total
Span (cm)	< 182	240	560	800
	≥ 182	60	140	200
	Total	300	700	1000

which is not very different from the earlier of the two tables in Section 3.3. Alternatively, and often more usefully (because the true probabilities are usually unknown), we can calculate expectations conditional on the margins of the table being exactly as in Section 3.3; then

$$Pr(A) = \frac{210}{1000}, \ Pr(B) = \frac{280}{1000},$$

and the 'short stature but long-armed' expectation on the hypothesis of independence is

$$1000 \times \frac{210}{1000} \times \frac{280}{1000} = 58.8.$$

An expected number need not be an integer; 'expected' here relates to an average in repeated samplings, not to any notion of the actual frequency 'most likely to occur'. The new table is

| | | Height (cm) | | |
		< 170	≥ 170	Total
Span (cm)	< 182	221.2	568.8	790.0
	≥ 182	58.8	151.2	210.0
	Total	280.0	720.0	1000

The first of the two tables in Section 3.3 agrees well with either of these, the second shows clearly the discrepancy arising from non-independence – height and arm-length are positively associated, as will be demonstrated convincingly by a test in Section 4.4.

Similarly we can speak of the expected number of white mice in a sample of 2 from a population consisting of 3 white, 2 brown. Since 2, 1, 0 white on average occur with frequencies in the proportions $3:6:1$,

$$\text{Expectation} = (3 \times 2 + 6 \times 1 + 1 \times 0)/(3 + 6 + 1) = 1.2,$$

alternatively written as E (number of white). The general result is

$$E(\text{number}) = \Sigma(\text{probability} \times \text{number}), \qquad [3.\text{III}]$$

where Σ means 'sum over all possible results'. Thus for the white mice

$$E(\text{number}) = \frac{3}{10} \times 2 + \frac{6}{10} \times 1 + \frac{1}{10} \times 0 = 1.2.$$

EXERCISES

3.1 Two unbiased cubical dice, with faces marked 1, 2, 3, 4, 5 and 6, are thrown. By consideration of all possibilities, find the probabilities that:

    (i) Neither shows a 2;

    (ii) The two show the same score;

    (iii) The total of the two is a perfect square;

    (iv) The difference of the two is an odd number.

3.2 Plant A gives 20 seeds, of which 8 would produce a plant with white flowers, 12 would produce red flowers. Plant B (of the same species) gives 70 seeds of which 42 would produce white flowers and 28 red. Every seed will germinate if sown. One plant is chosen by spin of a fair coin and one seed is selected from it at random. What is the probability that it will produce a red flower? Alternatively, the 90 seeds are thoroughly mixed and one randomly chosen seed is sown; what is the probability of a red flower? (These ideas have implications for natural selection: will each of a group of plants contribute equally to the next generation, or will those that yield more seeds be proportionately more represented?)

3.3 In a certain hospital, 60% of the patients are male, 40% are female.

The probability that a man is given a blood test is 0.15; the probability for a woman is 0.10. Find

(i) The probability that a randomly chosen patient is tested;
(ii) The probability that a randomly chosen record of a test relates to a woman.

(Compare with Exercise 2.4)

3.4 In a certain locality where the two native British species of oak are common, the probability that a randomly chosen oak is *Quercus robur* is 0.7, and that it is *Q. petraea* 0.3. An entomologist believes that the probabilities of infestation by a particular species of insect are 0.05 and 0.20, respectively, for the two oak species. Find

(i) The probability of infestation for a randomly chosen oak irrespective of species;
(ii) The probability that an oak tree randomly chosen among all those *infested* is *Q. petraea*.

3.5 A laboratory technician must prepare a large number of pieces of animal tissue for use in a certain technique. Each piece takes 20 minutes to prepare; there is then a probability 0.8 that it will be good for use and a probability 0.2 that it will be bad. Its quality cannot be recognized immediately, but two tests are available. Test A takes 10 minutes per piece and always distinguishes good from bad. Test B takes only 1 minute but is less trustworthy: a good piece has probability 0.05 of misclassification as bad and probability 0.20 of being described as doubtful, a bad piece has probability 0.10 of misclassification as good and probability 0.10 of being described as doubtful. If a good piece is discarded because it is thought bad, the 20 minutes of preparation have been wasted. If a bad piece is used because it is thought good, the consequence is disastrous and 200 minutes of effort are wasted.

Consider three policies, and advise on which will on average waste least time:

(i) Use all pieces without preliminary testing;
(ii) Use Test A on every piece and discard all that are bad;
(iii) Use Test B on every piece, accept all that appear good, discard all that appear bad, re-test all doubtful pieces with Test A.

If a proportion P_1 of pieces would 'cost' T_1 minutes and a proportion P_2 would cost T_2 minutes, where $P_1 + P_2 = 1$, the average cost per piece would be $(P_1 T_1 + P_2 T_2)$ minutes. This idea, which generalizes easily to more than 2 classes, is related to that of expectation introduced in Section 3.6; the average time per piece is the *expectation of time* or the *expected time* as explained further in Section 5.8. You are intended to find the expectation for each of (i), (ii) and (iii).

3.6 An X-ray machine used for diagnosing a disease present in about 10% of a population gives only 80% correct results. Thus it records 1000 persons as follows:

Machine record

True state	−	+	Total
Disease	20	80	100
Healthy	720	180	900

$(80 + 720$ in all are correctly classified). A statistician offers to make a simple and inexpensive modification that will ensure 90% correct results. What will he do and why is his offer refused?

3.7 A proportion 0.2 of one-year-old cows have a disease, although the disease will not become easily recognizable until they are two years old. A skin test is known to have a probability 0.8 of showing a positive reaction in a diseased animal and a probability 0.1 of showing positive in a healthy animal. A one-year-old cow, randomly selected from the whole population, is positive; show that the probability that she is diseased is 2/3.

Every animal found positive on test is given a drug that has a probability 0.7 of curing a diseased cow but has no effect on healthy cows. What is the probability that, despite having had the drug, a cow is diseased?

4 Significance, binomials, and χ^2

4.1 Null hypotheses

The ideas in Chapter 3 enable us to look objectively at the question raised in Section 1.4. Read again the description of the experiment; the twelve mice will be assumed to have been divided at random, a fair lottery deciding the five for the double dose. In the investigation of scientific phenomena, we often wish to start from a sceptical outlook, and to decline to believe in an effect unless its consistent appearance forces us to discard our scepticism. This accords with the everyday practice of assuming simplicity or a standard behaviour until evidence is strong that what we observe cannot be explained without some new element. Quantitative approach to this process requires more formality. For the mouse experiment, formulate a hypothesis relevant to causation:

'The extra dose of Gopain does not affect the survival time of mice'.

We call this the null hypothesis (NH); we shall develop various consequences of its truth, for use in examination of whether belief in its truth is tenable. If the NH is true, the 12 survival times do not depend on which treatment a mouse received, and the columns of Table 1.1 in which they occur are determined by the act of randomization. Every possible way of dividing the 12 into groups of 7 and 5 must have the same probability. From a well-known formula (see Appendix to Chapter 4), the total number of ways is 12!/7!5!, or 792, and therefore each has probability 1/792.

4.2 A significance test

Suppose the five values in the E column of Table 1.1 had been 3, 7, 1, 8, 4, with the remaining seven values (10, 14, 20, 8, 18, 9, 12) in D. We should have been inclined to argue that occurrence of all the five smallest values in E was very unlikely if the NH were true, and that therefore the NH is untenable. This would be quite logical. Of the 792 possible random divisions, only 2 give this most extreme result (2 because either of the two 8-day mice might be in E). The probability is therefore 2/792, or approximately 0.0025.

Now turn to the data in Table 1.1. Again only 2 of the possible randomizations put 4, 10, 7, 1, 8 into E, but, on any reasonable criterion, many others are equally or more extreme. For example 3, 10, 8, 1, 8 and 4, 10, 3, 1, 12 are equivalent in giving a mean of 6 (or a total of 30); others such as 3, 10, 4, 1, 9 and 3, 4, 7, 14, 1 give smaller totals and means. We might search the 792 possibilities to find *every* selection of 5 out of 12 that gives a total of 30 or less. With under 1000 possibilities in all, a systematic search is not difficult. It is tedious and requires great care, as I am aware from my first draft of this section in which I wrote '31', instead of the correct '33'. Therefore, the probability of a result at least as extreme as Table 1.1 is

$$33/792 = 1/24 = 0.042$$

if the NH is true, much larger than the previous 0.0025 but still quite small. A sufficiently small probability would justify rejection of the NH. For example, if someone asserted that during a year Vancouver is as likely as not to exceed Cairo in its total hours of sunshine, we would expect meteorological records for a period such as 50 years to confute him: if his hypothesis is true, the occurrence of 50 years out of 50 in which Cairo had the higher figure would have an exceedingly small probability (2^{-50}, or less than 10^{-15}). Indeed, a much shorter period such as 20 or even 10 years would give a probability small enough to convince most people. But what is 'sufficiently small'? A convention of using 0.05 is long established. The procedure is known as a *significance test* and the probability used is the *significance level*.

Choice of 0.05 as the significance level introduces a considerable risk that a null hypothesis is rejected even when it is true: if similar procedures are used regularly (without restriction to the same total number of observations), of tests made on null hypotheses that are true on average 1 in 20 will lead to rejection of the NH. To adopt a smaller probability (e.g. 0.01 or 0.002) is permissible, but greater protection against rejecting true hypotheses is bought at the price of reduced power to detect small genuine effects. At first sight, the arbitrariness of using 0.05 is disconcerting. Yet in daily life and in science we are surrounded by equally arbitrary conventions (the voltage for electrical supply, the dimensions of a lawn tennis court, the lengths of the 12 months, the division of the day into hours, minutes, seconds), which may have recognizable historical origins but which cannot claim any absolute basis of correctness. For significance tests, some standard is needed in order to provide comparability between applications in different contexts, and common sense suggests 0.001 to 0.1 as the reasonable range of choice. Particular circumstances or even a strong personal inclination, can justify a different significance level, but the departure from convention should be specified clearly. (To refer to, say, the 'University Students Association' by its initial letters is legitimate, but confusion may follow unless the abbreviation is explained!) The convention that 'statistically significant' refers to a significance level 0.05 (and that 'statistically highly significant' refers to 0.01) is general in scientific literature, and its acceptance here will avoid somewhat unprofitable argument. We thus reject the Gopain NH because 0.042 is less than 0.05: in the face of the results, we cannot reasonably continue to believe Gopain to be without effect. Had the calculated probability been 0.073 instead of 0.042, comparison with 0.05 would have given the conclusion 'not significant'. That would *not* have been interpreted as a proof that Gopain had no effect on survival time, but only that any effect existing is too small to be detected without more data. We do not use our arbitrary significance level to 'dichotomize' null hypotheses into false and true; rather do we regard them as indicators of which null hypotheses are clearly now unacceptable and which are still consistent with the available data.

The conclusion may depend substantially on how the phrase 'more extreme' is interpreted. For example, we might have noted that the four longest survivals occurred in D, and then based a test on the probability that a specified set of 7 out of 12 should include the 4 largest values. The number of ways of choosing 7 out of 12 when 4 of the 7 are fixed is the number of ways of choosing the remaining 3 out of 8 or $8!/3!5!$. This leads to a probability $56/792$ or 0.07, not statistically significant. Such a procedure is less sensitive to small departures from the NH, since it does not make full use of all values. Other possibilities can be suggested. The method I have described is not a very practical way of testing, except for small numbers of observations, because the systematic counting of possibilities can be very laborious. I shall turn to alternatives later.

4.3 Binomial frequency distribution

Chapter 3 examined various questions relating to an observation that can have either of two outcomes. Supposing we have a probability structure defined in this manner and we ask further questions about more complicated events. For example:

(i) In 20 spins of a fair coin, what is the probability of exactly 14 Heads?

(ii) In 20 spins, what is the probability of *at least* 14 Heads?

(iii) In 60 throws of a perfect cubical die, what is the probability that 6 appears at most twice?

These are typical questions in relation to games of chance and gambling. Similar but more complicated problems have been studied in relation to bridge, poker, and other games. Our concern is with biological investigations, such as:

(iv) Maize seed is sold as giving 90% germination. What is the probability that in a test sample of 200 fewer than 170 germinate? (Here is a basis for a legal requirement on quality).

(v) A genetic character, A, in mice is thought to be such that the probability of its appearance in any one mouse born of specified parents is $\frac{1}{4}$. If 20 offspring are raised, what is the probability that at most 2 have the character? (Here is a basis for a test of a genetic hypothesis).

Examine the last example a little more thoroughly. For simplicity, look at the smaller problem of 5 offspring with at most 2 being A. I discuss only independent individuals, and disregard the complication of identical twins, etc. Consider the probability of a sequence such as

$$\times \times A \times A,$$

for which the rule of independence (Section 3.3) gives the probability

$$\left(\frac{3}{4}\right)\left(\frac{3}{4}\right)\left(\frac{1}{4}\right)\left(\frac{3}{4}\right)\left(\frac{1}{4}\right) = \left(\frac{1}{4}\right)^2\left(\frac{3}{4}\right)^3.$$

Although the factors come in different orders, the same probability would apply to any other particular sequence with exactly two A's, such as

$$A \times \times \times A.$$

There are altogether (Appendix to Chapter 4)

$$\binom{5}{2} = \frac{5!}{2!3!} = 10$$

alternative sequences, and because these are mutually exclusive the probabilities can be added. We can list systematically all the 2^5 possibilities; one way of doing so is to introduce A into each possible position as shown below:

1.	×	×	×	×	×
2.	A	×	×	×	×
3.	×	A	×	×	×
4.	A	A	×	×	×
5.	×	×	A	×	×
6.	A	×	A	×	×
7.	×	A	A	×	×

.
.
.

32.	A	A	A	A	A

Then count in how many sequences A occurs r times:

$r =$	0	1	2	3	4	5
no. of sequences	1	5	10	10	5	1

A quicker route to the answer uses the formula for the number of ways of having A r times and not-A $(5 - r)$ times, and leads to

$$Pr(\text{A appears } r \text{ times}) = \frac{5!}{r!(5 - r)!}\left(\frac{1}{4}\right)^r\left(\frac{3}{4}\right)^{5 - r}.$$

From here, we can easily step to the more general result for n mice with P in place of $1/4$ as the probability of A:

$$Pr(\text{A appears } r \text{ times in } n) = \frac{n!}{r!(n - r)!}P^r(1 - P)^{n - r}. \quad [4.\text{I}]$$

This important result is known as the *binomial distribution of probability*. The name is given because of a close relation with the binomial theorem (Appendix to Chapter 4). The probability that the event A appears r times in n trials corresponds with the term in $Q^{n - r}P^r$ in the binomial expansion of $(Q + P)^n$, where Q is eventually replaced by $(1 - P)$. The number of 'successes', that is to say occurrences of A, must be one of the integers $0, 1, 2, \ldots, (n - 1), n$. The binomial distribution shows how the total probability, 1.0, is *distributed* among these mutually exclusive possibilities. Essential conditions are that the n trials are completely independent of one another and that the probability of A is constant (P) throughout.

From Equation [4.I], we quickly obtain the answers to the problems stated earlier:

(i) Pr (14 H in 20 spins) $= \dfrac{20!}{14!6!}\left(\dfrac{1}{2}\right)^{14}\left(\dfrac{1}{2}\right)^{6} = \dfrac{20!}{14!6!}\left(\dfrac{1}{2}\right)^{20}$

$$= 0.0370;$$

(ii) Pr (14 or more H in 20 spins) $= \sum\limits_{r=14}^{r=20} \dfrac{20!}{r!(20-r)!}\left(\dfrac{1}{2}\right)^{20}$, where

'$\sum$' means 'take the sum of' for all the stated values of r;

(iii) Pr (at most 2 sixes in 60 throws)

$$= \sum\limits_{r=0}^{r=2} \dfrac{60!}{r!(60-r)!}\left(\dfrac{1}{6}\right)^{r}\left(\dfrac{5}{6}\right)^{60-r};$$

(iv) Pr (fewer than 170 in 200 germinate)

$$= \sum\limits_{r=0}^{r=169} \dfrac{200!}{r!(200-r)!}(0.9)^{r}(0.1)^{200-r}, \text{ where } 0.9 \text{ is the pro-}$$

bability equivalent to 90% germination;

(v) Pr (A occurs twice or less in 20) $= \sum\limits_{0}^{2} \dfrac{20!}{r!(20-r)!}\left(\dfrac{1}{4}\right)^{r}\left(\dfrac{3}{4}\right)^{20-r}$

$$= \left(\dfrac{3}{4}\right)^{20} + 20\left(\dfrac{1}{4}\right)\left(\dfrac{3}{4}\right)^{19} + 190\left(\dfrac{1}{4}\right)^{2}\left(\dfrac{3}{4}\right)^{18}$$

$$= \left(\dfrac{3}{4}\right)^{18}\left(\dfrac{9}{16} + \dfrac{60}{16} + \dfrac{190}{16}\right)$$

$$= \dfrac{259}{16}\left(\dfrac{3}{4}\right)^{18}$$

$$= 0.0913.$$

You need not worry about completion of the arithmetic above; the important point is to understand the logic of the formulae, from which stage a computer or even a pocket calculator readily completes the labour. I have shown (v) in some detail because it reduces to a calculation that is easily finished by logarithms. When numbers are large, approximations are available; these make use of continuous variate ideas, to which we turn in Chapter 5. As an extension to (v), we might wish to know 'How many offspring must I raise in order that probability of 3 or more A mice shall be at least 0.97?'. Evidently 20 is not enough, for this gives probability $1 - 0.0913$, or 0.9087, to 3 or more. Trial and error, or special tables, show that 26 is the least number.

I hope that elementary mathematics has made you familiar with the Σ notation. Suppose that $f(r)$ is any function of the integer r, that is to say any quantity numerically determinate when r is specified [such as r^3 or $\log(r + 1)$]. The notation

$$\sum_{r=3}^{r=7}$$

means 'Take the sum of whatever follows, evaluated for $r = 3, 4, 5, 6, 7$ (all integers from 3 to 7 inclusive)'. Hence

$$\sum_{r=3}^{r=7} f(r) = f(3) + f(4) + f(5) + f(6) + f(7),$$

and as particular examples

$$\sum_{r=3}^{r=7} r^2 = 3^2 + 4^2 + 5^2 + 6^2 + 7^2,$$

$$\sum_{r=3}^{r=7} (r - 6) = (3 - 6) + (4 - 6) + (5 - 6) + (6 - 6) + (7 - 6),$$

$$\sum_{r=2}^{r=9} 19 = 19 + 19 + 19 + 19 + 19 + 19 + 19 + 19.$$

Note the last particularly! The number 19 is unaltered by the value of r, but still Σ tells us to add it the appropriate number of times. Again

$$\sum_{r=1}^{r=n} r = 1 + 2 + 3 + \ldots + n.$$

Note that if c is a constant value independent of r ($c = 25$ or $c = -5.71$ or $c = \pi$)

$$\sum cf(r) = c\sum f(r)$$

whatever the limits of summation:

$$\sum_{r=3}^{r=7} \pi r^2 = \pi(3^2 + 4^2 + 5^2 + 6^2 + 7^2).$$

When there is no doubt about what is being summed, we often simplify the Σ notation and write

$$\sum_{r=3}^{7} \quad \text{or even} \quad \sum_{3}^{7} \quad \text{or merely} \quad \sum.$$

Note also that

$$\sum_{4}^{26}(r^2 + 5r) = \sum_{4}^{26}r^2 + \sum_{4}^{26}5r$$

$$= \sum_{4}^{26}r^2 + 5\sum_{4}^{26}r$$

and similar results. All these bits of notation are helpful in numerical exercises.

4.4 The χ^2 test

We often need to assess whether a series of observed frequencies deviate from what a theory predicts to an extent that renders the theory implausible. The logic is similar to that of Sections 4.1 and 4.2. Consider examples (iv) and (v) above. Is occurrence of only 2 mice of type A in 20 evidence that justifies rejecting the null hypothesis that $Pr(A) = 1/4$ for individual mice? Is germination of only 170 seeds out of 200 justification for rejecting the null hypothesis that a batch of seed has 90% germination? Calculations in Section 4.3 showed that the probability of 2 A-mice or fewer in 20 is 0.09, a value greater than 0.05 and thus not indicating statistical significance for the scarcity of type A. No proof that $Pr(A) = 1/4$ is implied, but only absence of strong evidence against this value. The conclusion would have been the same had the null hypothesis stated a probability of 0.20 instead of 0.25, or 0.18 or 0.27, etc., and not all can be true.

For larger numbers, as in the seed question, similar arithmetic may demand excessive labour because so many binomial terms must be calculated. Fortunately, mathematical theory (at a level far beyond what can be explained here) shows that an entirely different and simpler calculation can lead to a good approximation to the required probability. This involves a quantity known as χ^2 (pronounced 'ky-squared'). First record observed and expected frequencies, expectations being calculated from the theoretical probability of 0.9 ($nP = 200 \times 0.9 = 180$):

	Germinate	Fail	Total
Observed (O)	170	30	200
Expected (E)	180	20	200
O − E	− 10	10	

Now calculate

$$\chi^2 = \sum \frac{(|O - E| - \frac{1}{2})^2}{E} \qquad [4.\text{II}]$$

where the summation is over the two classes of Germinate and Fail and $|O - E|$ means the absolute value irrespective of sign:

$$\chi^2 = \frac{(10 - \frac{1}{2})^2}{180} + \frac{(10 - \frac{1}{2})^2}{20}$$
$$= 0.501 + 4.512 = 5.01.$$

Obviously the larger the discrepancy of O from E the larger will χ^2 be. A theoretically derived probability that, when the null hypothesis is true, the value of χ^2 would be at least as large as that found can then be read from a table. Provided that the number of observations is reasonably large, this probability will approximate very closely to the exact result from the summation of binomial terms. Many text books omit the '$-\frac{1}{2}$' used in the calculation, and the omission makes little difference for large frequencies. However, this so-called continuity correction usually improves the approximation, and with a modern calculator its neglect saves no time.

Table 4.1 is extracted from much larger tables that exist, and is adequate for present purposes. Ignore for the present everything after the line for '1 degree of freedom'. The table tells the numerical value that will be exceeded with each of a selection of probabilities. In particular, 3.84 will be exceeded with probability 0.05, and the probability associated with 5.01 will therefore be substantially smaller. Note that the manner of calculating χ^2 is such as to give equal attention to deviations in either direction; 190 germinating and 10 failing would also have given 5.01. Often a scientist is equally interested in deviations in each direction (e.g. in examining genetic segregations). Here, however, the only concern is that of whether the quality of seed falls below the guarantee of 90% germination. Consequently, the probabilities in Table 4.1 should be read as half those shown, so that 2.71 should replace 3.84 as the critical value in the significance test. This distinction between '2-tail' and '1-tail' tests

Table 4.1 Probability levels for the χ^2 test

Degrees of freedom	Probability				
	0.50	0.10	0.05	0.02	0.01
1	0.45	2.71	3.84	5.41	6.64
2	1.4	4.6	6.0	7.8	9.2
3	2.4	6.3	7.8	9.8	11.3
4	3.4	7.8	9.5	11.7	13.3

is logically rather subtle, and a beginner should not worry much about it until he has advanced far enough to ask a statistician for a full explanation.

You are not expected to know anything about the theory of χ^2, but you may be helped by a little explanation of values such as 3.84 and 2.71. In principle, you could study these experimentally for yourself: all you need is a few pieces of card, simple arithmetic, and an enormous amount of time. If you do not have the time, you must *either* satisfy yourself on the basic idea and believe my account of what happens *or* learn enough mathematics to understand proofs that can be found in more advanced textbooks. For the numerical example above, take 10 identical pieces of card, say 3 cm × 3 cm, and mark one of them 'F'. Selecting one card at random will then be analogous to testing one seed. If the card is blank (probability 0.9), the seed germinates; if it has the mark 'F' (probability 0.1), it fails to germinate. Now determine results corresponding to 200 seeds. That is to say, pick a card and note the result, mix all 10 cards again, pick a second card at random and note the result, mix all 10 cards, pick a third, and so on until 200 results have been noted. Suppose F occurs 14 times and blank 186 times. As above, the expected numbers are 20, 180. Apply Equation [4.II]:

$$\chi^2 = \frac{(|-6| - 0.5)^2}{180} + \frac{(|6| - 0.5)^2}{20}$$

$$= (5.5)^2 \left(\frac{1}{180} + \frac{1}{20} \right)$$

$$= 1.68.$$

The selection of cards and calculation should not take you more than, say, 15 minutes. Now repeat the whole process 10 000 times; you will improve with practice, and a year of 40-hour weeks should suffice! You will find that of the 10 000 values of χ^2 the proportion exceeding 3.84 will be about 0.05; the proportion exceeding 2.71 will be about 0.1, and 6.64 will be exceeded by a proportion 0.01. These are not exact, but are good approximations. A great merit of the theoretical approach is that the same numbers (3.84, 2.71, 6.64, etc.) apply to experiments with a different probability or a different number of seeds tested. If the probability of germination were 0.85, you would need a new experimental study, taking 20 cards and marking 'F' on 3 of them (3/20 = 0.15); if 144 seeds were tested, the expectations would be 122.4 germinating and 21.6 'F'. The calculation of χ^2 follows the same formula, but again a vast number of repetitions would be needed. Except for small numbers, exact probability calculations as in Section 4.3 are also intolerably laborious for routine use; the approximate test of significance based on the quick calculation of χ^2 is therefore generally adopted.

The same test can be applied to tables such as those in Section 3.3. Expectations were calculated in the second table of Section 3.6. Hence we have for the imaginary observations in the first table of Section 3.3:

Height	Span	O	E	O − E	$\dfrac{(\lvert O - E\rvert - \frac{1}{2})^2}{E}$
< 170	< 182	224	221.2	2.8	0.024
< 170	⩾ 182	56	58.8	− 2.8	0.090
⩾ 170	< 182	566	568.8	− 2.8	0.009
⩾ 170	⩾ 182	154	151.2	2.8	0.035
					0.158

Note that all values of (O − E) must be equal in magnitude, but two are positive and two negative because of the requirement that the tables in Sections 3.3 and 3.6 should agree in row totals and in column totals. The result $\chi^2 = 0.16$, is well below 3.84, and thus the data show no serious departure from the proportionality of frequencies on which the expectations were based. As pointed out in Section 3.3, for the measurements under discussion, real life is much more likely to produce a table like the second one:

Height	Span	O	E	O − E	$\dfrac{(\lvert O - E\rvert - \frac{1}{2})^2}{E}$
< 170	< 182	264	221.2	42.8	8.09
< 170	⩾ 182	16	58.8	− 42.8	30.43
⩾ 170	< 182	526	568.8	− 42.8	3.15
⩾ 170	⩾ 182	194	151.2	42.8	11.83
					53.50

The enormous χ^2 leaves no doubts about statistical significance. The null hypothesis that the probability of short span is independent of whether measured for tall men or for short is firmly rejected.

Problems of this kind also could be examined by artificial sampling from pieces of marked card, but the process is more complicated than before. Take 1000 cards, mark 280 'S' for short, 720 'T' for tall. Mix well and withdraw a random sample of 210 cards (no replacement). These are the large spans, and the numbers of S and T among them can be counted. Suppose 43 are S; this gives the table

237	553	790
43	167	210
280	720	1000

Return the 210 cards, mix again and withdraw a new sample of 210. Again repeat 10 000 times, and calculate χ^2 as above for each of the 10 000 tables obtained. The proportion that exceeds 3.84 will again be about 0.05. As with the previous problem, theory proves that the χ^2 test gives a good approximation to this impracticable procedure.

4.5* Larger frequency tables

The χ^2 test has many other uses. One important feature is that it generalizes easily to larger tables of frequencies. For example, genetical theory might predict that seedlings from a cross between two plants will show a $1:2:1$ segregation for flower colour, and a classification of 286 independent seedlings might show:

	Red	Pink	White	Total
Observed (O)	52	168	66	286
Expected (E)	71.5	143.0	71.5	286

Here the expectations have been formed as $286 \times \frac{1}{4}$, $286 \times \frac{1}{2}$, $286 \times \frac{1}{4}$. This is analogous to the seed germination table. Analogous to the two-way table for height and span, one might have records from a study of a species of migrant bird. Perhaps in one year nestlings were ringed in four different colonies and a year later the numbers of ringed birds recovered were recorded as follows:

	Colony				
	A	B	C	D	Total
Recovered	30	75	24	31	160
Not recovered	150	225	63	202	640
Total	180	300	87	233	800

The null hypothesis now is that the probability of recovery is the same for all colonies. In order to calculate expectations, we note that the overall recovery rate was 160/800 or 0.2, and we apply this proportion to the total for each colony:

	Colony				
	A	B	C	D	Total
Recovered	36.0	60.0	17.4	46.6	160
Not recovered	144.0	240.0	69.6	186.4	640
Total	180	300	87	233	800

For either table,

$$\chi^2 = \Sigma \frac{(O - E)^2}{E}$$

where summation is over every class of the observed frequencies. Note that '$-\frac{1}{2}$' is appropriate only to the small tables in Section 4.4 and must not be used here. Hence for the flower colours

$$\chi^2 = \frac{19.5^2}{71.5} + \frac{25.0^2}{143.0} + \frac{5.5^2}{71.5} = 10.1,$$

and for the bird recoveries

$$\chi^2 = \frac{6.0^2}{36.0} + \frac{15.0^2}{60.0} + \frac{6.6^2}{17.4} + \frac{15.6^2}{46.6} + \frac{6.0^2}{150.0} + \frac{15.0^2}{240.0} + \frac{6.6^2}{69.6} + \frac{15.6^2}{186.4}$$
$$= 15.6.$$

Because more classes are involved, the values of χ^2 corresponding to different probabilities are increased. If the table of observed frequencies has C columns and R rows (exclusive of totals), χ^2 is said to have $(C - 1)(R - 1)$ *degrees of freedom*. For the genetic problem, $C = 3$ (3 colours of flowers or 3 genotypes) and $R = 1$; for the birds, $C = 4$ (colonies) and $R = 2$ (recovered or not). Hence 10.1 is to be compared with 6.0 in Table 4.1 (i.e. 2 degrees of freedom) and 15.6 is to be compared with 7.8. In both instances, the calculated χ^2 exceeds the value tabulated for probability 0.05; the hypotheses that flower colour rests simply on a $1:2:1$ segregation and that recoveries of ringed birds occur independently of colony are therefore both rejected.

With extended versions of Table 4.1, the method of testing can be used for still larger tables. For example, the bird-ringing investigation might have distinguished between birds recovered at the colony of origin, birds recovered elsewhere, and birds not recovered. The only conditions are that the frequencies must relate to independent individuals and that no expectation is very small.

4.6* The Poisson distribution

An important extreme form of the binomial distribution arises when the probability P is very small but the number of trials is very large. For example, a system of trapping animals (or birds or insects, or fungal spores) may have a very small probability of any particular individual being caught but the number of members of the species exposed to the chance of catching is large and the expected number caught, nP, is of moderate size. The probabilities that the observed number caught shall be 0, 1, 2, . . . are (in the limit for small P, large n) proportional to

$$1, m, \frac{m^2}{2!}, \frac{m^3}{3!}, \frac{m^4}{4!}, \cdots$$

where m is written for nP.[†] Essential conditions for this result are that the individuals in the population have equal probabilities of capture and are independent of one another. Thus it will not apply if some animals are actively foraging while others rarely leave their 'dens', or if insects are moving in swarms. The name, Poisson distribution, refers to an association with an eighteenth century French mathematician.

The ideal conditions are sometimes fulfilled, and the distribution is a reference standard for examining whether observations depart markedly from randomness. Perhaps stored fruit is liable to insect damage and questions arise as to whether the insects enter fruits entirely at random, whether mutual avoidance leads to a more uniform attack, or whether there is some grouping of attacks manifested by an excess of heavily damaged and undamaged fruit with a corresponding deficiency of moderate damage. Examination of 150 fruits gives

Insects per fruit	0	1	2	3	4	5	6	> 6
No. of fruit	32	54	34	21	6	2	1	0
'Proportional values'	1.00	1.50	1.13	0.56	0.21	0.06	0.02	0.00
Expectations	33.5	50.2	37.8	18.8	7.0	2.0	0.7	0.0

[†]The sum of these quantities is well known in mathematics as being e^m, where $e = 2.718\ 281\ 8\ldots$ (a constant used as the base of natural logarithms).

There are in all

$$54 \times 1 + 24 \times 2 + 21 \times 3 + \ldots + 1 \times 6 = 225$$

insects, and therefore m, the mean number per fruit is estimated as $225/150 = 1.50$. Immediately below the observed frequencies is written the sequence of the previous paragraph

$$1, 1.50, (1.50)^2/2!, \text{ and so on.}$$

The total of these is 4.48, and to obtain expected frequencies totalling 150 we must multiply each of them by 150/4.48.

Comparison of the observed and expected frequencies shows a good agreement. Once again χ^2 can be used to assess the probability of a set of deviations at least as extreme as those observed occurring by chance. Because of the small expectations, it is advisable to group together '4 and over', to give 9 observed and 9.7 expected. Calculation of χ^2 by the standard formula is left as an exercise for the reader; 5 columns of observations are used, and therefore there are 4 degrees of freedom. The χ^2 will be smaller than 9.2, and therefore the evidence is insufficient to reject the NH that insects attack fruit at random and independently of one another.

Appendix to Chapter 4

You should be aware that the number of ways of dividing n objects into a group of r and a group of $(n - r)$ is

$$\frac{n!}{r!\,(n-r)!},$$

where $n!$ (read as 'factorial n') is an abbreviation for the product $n(n - 1)(n - 2)\ldots3 \times 2 \times 1$. This expression is so important that it has several special symbols; I shall refer to it as $\binom{n}{r}$, but $_nC_r$ is also common. Note that $\binom{n}{r}$ and $\binom{n}{n-r}$ are necessarily equal. Also $\binom{n}{1} = n$ follows immediately from the definition. In order to maintain consistence with the general rule $n! = n(n - 1)!$, it appears that 0! must be interpreted as 1 (for take $n = 1$), and therefore also $\binom{n}{0} = 1$.

The *binomial theorem* states that, for any integer n,

$$(a + b)^n = a^n + \binom{n}{1}a^{n-1}b + \binom{n}{2}a^{n-2}b^2 + \ldots$$
$$+ \binom{n}{r}a^{n-r}b^r + \ldots + b^n.$$

If you are not familiar with this, write it out in full for $n = 2$ and $n = 3$, to give results that you ought to recognize. Thus $(a + b)^n$ is expressed as the sum of all terms of the form $\binom{n}{r}a^{n-r}b^r$, starting from $r = 0$ and continuing to $r = n$.

For small values of n and r, $\binom{n}{r}$ is easily constructed from the so-called *Pascal Triangle*:

r \ n	0	1	2	3	4	5	6
1	1	1	0				
2	1	2	1	0			
3	1	3	3	1	0		
4	1	4	6	4	1	0	
5	1	5	10	10	5	1	0

Each entry in this table is the sum of the two numbers on the line above that are respectively north-west and north of it ($3 + 3 = 6$, $4 + 6 = 10$, etc.).

EXERCISES

In Exercises 4.1–4.5, you are asked about the probability of some compound event, and you are invited to consider obtaining this by use of the binomial distribution. Assume that P is a known numerical value; if it makes the questions easier for you, use the values suggested in round brackets. Your answer should be *either* an expression from which the required probability can be calculated (you need not complete the arithmetic) *or* an explanation of why the binomial distribution is not applicable.

4.1 A gardener grows large numbers of red and white carnations. The probability is P (perhaps $P = \frac{1}{4}$?) that a randomly chosen plant is red-flowered. Starting at a randomly chosen plant, he picks all available blooms along a row until he has a bunch of 50 flowers. What is the probability that his bunch includes at least 10 red?

4.2 A cubical die has a probability, P, of showing '6' when thrown ($P = 1/6$?). Find the probability of scoring 6 at least 5 times in six independent throws.

4.3 The probability that a ewe produces twins is P ($P = 0.35$?). Find the probability that a majority of a flock of 55 ewes have twins.

4.4 In a certain human population, the probability that a single eye (adult) is brown is P ($P = 0.6$?). Find the probability that the total of 20 eyes in a random sample of 10 men includes at most 4 brown eyes.

4.5 A library binds all its books in black or red, with a proportion P in red ($P = 0.3$?). A reader selects 5 books strictly at random. What is the probability that he has an odd number of red books?

4.6 A large population of animals includes 1% carrying a certain disease. Although diseased animals are not directly recognizable, a diagnostic test can be applied to any animal. An investigator searching for diseased animals proposes to take animals at random, test each, and class as diseased all that yield a positive result. Unfortunately the test is far from perfect: for diseased animals, the probability of a positive test is 0.9, but a non-diseased animal has a probability 0.2 of appearing positive on test. Show that, among animals that the investigator describes as diseased, the probability of disease is 0.043. Show that insistence on two independent positive test results per animal increases this probability (that an animal *said* to be diseased *is* diseased) only to 0.17.

4.7 The probabilities that a new-born female of a certain animal species will eventually have 0, 1, 2 daughters are 1/5, 3/5, 1/5. Find the probabilities that:

   (i) 2 females between them produce *at least* 1 daughter;
   (ii) 3 females among them produce *exactly* 3 daughters in all;
   (iii) 1 female has no sons but at least 1 *grand*-daughter.

(Answer by systematic listing of possibilities and applying rules already discussed.)

4.8 A sample of blood is taken from a cat and 80 red cells are examined; 8 show a specific abnormality. The cat is given regular doses of a new drug for two weeks, after which a new sample of blood is taken; of 120 red cells, 33 show the abnormality. Use χ^2 to test the hypothesis that the population proportion of abnormal cells was the same before and after the drug, and express your conclusions in words.

4.9 A plant breeder needs at least 5 plants with double flowers from a cross that has probabilities $\frac{1}{2}$, $\frac{1}{2}$ for producing progeny with single and double flowers respectively. He has two options:

    (i) He will himself care for 16 seedlings until they flower;

or

    (ii) His not very competent assistant will care for 24 seedl-
ings: the probability that a seedling dies before flowering
is then 1/3, irrespective of flower type.

For each option state exactly the computations needed to
determine the probabilities of success in obtaining at least 5
plants with double flowers. *Do not* attempt the arithmetic, but
show what quantities must be summed and over what ranges of
summation. How would you use the results of the two
calculations to advise the plant breeder on his choice of option?

4.10 From a large sowing of seed, 480 plants are raised, and are
classified for flower colour and leaf type:

Leaf	Dark blue	Light blue	Yellow	Pink	White	Total
Rough	41	105	36	39	151	372
Smooth	3	15	18	28	44	108
	44	120	54	67	195	480

Form a table of expected frequencies on the null hypothesis that
colour and leaf type are independent and complete a χ^2 test.

4.11 A psychologist tests co-ordination of hand and eye in 475
subjects. He finds that 30 can perform a certain task with the
right hand but not the left, 13 with the left but not the right.
What light does this throw on whether success rates for the two
hands differ in the population sampled? Is any further information needed? State and test any appropriate null hypothesis.

4.12 Fertilization of the flowers of a certain plant was carefully
controlled so as to give seeds (all looking alike) that have
probabilities $\frac{1}{4}, \frac{1}{2}, \frac{1}{4}$ of producing new plants with red, pink and
white flowers respectively. Four randomly chosen seeds pro-
duce plants that are all grown to flowering. Find the probabilities that:

    (i) the first two plants are white flowered, the third red, and
the fourth pink;

    (ii) two plants are pink and two non-pink (irrespective of
order);

    (iii) at least two plants are pink.

Suppose that you were to grow *n* plants (instead of 4). What is the probability that all are white? You wish to obtain at least one non-white plant. Show that $n = 5$ will make the probability of this more than 0.999.

4.13 Theory suggests that on average one-quarter of the cells from a particular source will have a specified property Q. From a well mixed suspension of cells 30 are taken and of these 3 are of type Q. Explain the use of the binomial probability distribution to calculate, using the null hypothesis expressed by the theory, the probability of so small a number of Q-cells occurring by chance. (You need not complete the arithmetic.)

5 Continuous variates

5.1 Statistical inference

We have looked at some *deductive* problems, for example, in Chapter 4 where we supposed a simple probability to be known and we based on it a more complicated calculation. Genetics abounds in situations where we know (or believe we know) the probability of an elementary event – say birth of a tailless mouse – and we want to derive the probability of a compound event – say occurrence of at least 2 tailless mice in a litter of 8. Games of chance provide other illustrations, as is evident from some of my references to coins and dice. Deductive reasoning, from general rule to particular instance, is essential to many applications of science. The physician uses his knowledge of the general properties of a micro-organism to decide how to treat a particular patient; the engineer uses his knowledge of physical characteristics of his materials to determine the requirements of a particular bridge. Advancement of science, however, calls for *induction* from the particular to the general. Whether we think of the laws of gravity or the laws of genetics, general formulation arose as an attempt to fit particular observations into a coherent framework. In quantitative biology, familiarity with deductive processes is an essential foundation for inductive reasoning, but more is required both in logical outlook and in statistical technique. In relation to the two versions of the Gopain problem (Sections 1.2 and 1.4), we have already encountered the central question: given observational or experimental data from a sample, what can be said about the population from which the sample is drawn?

A great part of all science is concerned with inference from the particular to the general. The chemist, from tests with quite small quantities of a compound, infers that certain properties are possessed by every conceivable sample of the compound and therefore by the population. Why else do we assert confidently that all H_2SO_4 has the same properties, totally different from those of NaCl? So the biologist, from the relatively few specimens of a new plant or animal species that he sees, infers that certain characteristics are general to the species. *Statistical inference* is concerned with properties that vary between individuals. We do not need statistics to describe the fact that all *Drosophila melanogaster* have 6 legs or that all *Taraxacum officinale* have yellow flowers. If we want to describe numbers of eggs laid by individual *D. melanogaster*, weights of dry matter in plants of *T. officinale*, meat yields of sheep under stated conditions of management, or the change in duration of life for men or mice after receiving a certain drug, we cannot escape from statistical inference: records will be obtainable from a fairly small number of individuals, and we must try to derive valid statements about the population. Commonly, but not always, greatest importance attaches to statements about mean values for the population. Any numerical statement that purports to relate to the population is essentially statistical.

Three major categories of statistical inference are:

(i) *Estimation*: obtaining a value for a numerical property of a population and assessing the trustworthiness of this estimate (What is the mean number of eggs laid by a female *Drosophila*? By how much is the mean weight of a rat that receives a protein supplement for 10 weeks after weaning greater than that of a rat on a standard diet?);

(ii) *Hypothesis testing*: testing whether two (or more) samples from a population that have been treated differently can reasonably be supposed unaffected by treatment differences in respect of specified properties (Is the meat yield of sheep affected by allowing them to graze on an 'improved' pasture?);

(iii) *Planning further research*: questions on how many observations to make, and topics known as design of experiments and of sampling studies (In Section 1.4, how many mice are needed in order that the experiment shall make a reasonably sensitive test of the hypothesis, and how should these be allocated to single and double doses?).

Because (i) and (ii) are closely connected, I discuss them first; indeed Section 4.2 illustrated hypothesis testing, but consideration of continuous variates will extend and clarify the ideas. Experimental design, an intrinsically interesting topic, cannot easily be presented without the background of (i) and (ii), and I defer it until Chapter 8. Another important category of inference is *decision theory*, the devising of rules for optimal decision in the face of uncertainty. Scientific research is concerned with developing and modifying hypotheses, not with any absolute 'decision' that a statement is true. In scientific and industrial technology, decisions that certain processes or courses of action are 'best' (perhaps least costly, most profitable, or quickest) can be imperative. Exercise 3.5 illustrates this for a very elementary problem, but I shall not be able to discuss the topic at all generally.

5.2 Distribution function

These considerations of inference are relevant to discrete and continuous variates. Chapter 4 has illustrated inference by hypothesis testing for discrete variates, a valuable logical process but one that at first encounter may appear to a biologist as very arbitrary. Attention will now turn to the understanding of continuous variates, in which context estimation is more easily explained and compared with significance tests.

A typical continuous variate is weight or height. For example, adult male weights perhaps range from 40 kg to 120 kg (of course, even greater extremes are known) and any value such as 71.543... kg is possible (with the number of digits limited only by the accuracy of the weighing instrument). The times in Table 1.1 are of this kind; they are recorded only to the nearest day, but special consequences of this are not of great importance. Any continuous variate can easily be transformed into a binomial variate. We need only classify weights dichotomously (i.e. into two distinct groups) as, for example, ' $\leqslant 65$ kg' and ' > 65 kg', or jaundice after ' $\leqslant 7$ days' and ' > 7 days'. To replace series D of Table 1.1 by the record: '1 patient $\leqslant 7$ days, 6 patients > 7 days' is to sacrifice information; such a step is sometimes useful for a condensed summary, or as part of a rapid approximate analysis, but we usually prefer to work with the actual values of the variate.

We can extend this idea. For a continuous variate, y, we can think of many different dichotomies of the data. Thus weights of men might be divided at 65 kg, 70 kg, 75 kg, ..., or even at 66.0 kg, 66.1 kg, 66.2 kg, ... If we knew all the individual weights in the population, we could classify each person according to whether or not he was in the lower class relative to as many points of division as we choose to use. If the symbol Y represents the weight of a man to be chosen at random from the population, from the relative frequencies we can determine $Pr(Y \leqslant 65)$, $Pr(Y \leqslant 66.2)$, $Pr(Y \leqslant 70)$, etc. With any choice we like to make of a value y at which to dichotomize the population, we have a probability $Pr(Y \leqslant y)$. Since any man who is less than 65 kg in weight must be less than 66 kg and so on, $Pr(Y \leqslant y)$ must increase as y increases. For any specified population, this probability is a function of y, that is a numerical value uniquely determined by y. It is often written

$$F(y) = Pr(Y \leqslant y), \qquad [5.I]$$

and is known as the *cumulative distribution function* of y. It must satisfy

$$0 \leqslant F(y) \leqslant 1 \quad \text{for all } y, \qquad [5.II]$$

and its non-decreasing property means that

$$\text{if} \quad y_1 < y_2, \quad \text{then} \quad F(y_1) \leqslant F(y_2). \qquad [5.III]$$

(These are merely mathematical forms of statements that $F(y)$ is a probability and that it cannot decrease as y increases.) Figure 5.1 illustrates a possible form of curve that may result when $F(y)$ is plotted against y.

For a discrete variate, a distribution function can be defined in exactly the same way; it cannot have a similarly smooth shape and will appear graphically as what is termed a step-function (Figure 5.2). Suppose that we knew all the probabilities corresponding to the

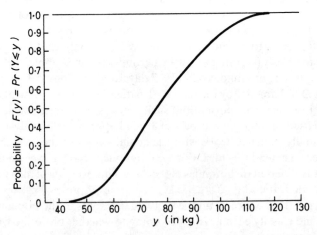

Figure 5.1. A possible cumulative distribution function for heights of adult males.

population of 'days to jaundice' corresponding to the sample in series D of Table 1.1. The only possible values for Y are $0, 1, 2, 3, \ldots$. Consequently, for example,

$$Pr(Y \leqslant 11.9) = Pr(Y \leqslant 11.6) = Pr(Y \leqslant 11.271) = Pr(Y \leqslant 11.0);$$

since Y is an integer, if it is less than 12 it cannot exceed 11. Hence $F(y)$ jumps upwards at each integer, but is flat between integers. For this variate, we could envisage presence or absence of jaundice being recorded hourly instead of daily, in which event each large step would be replaced by 24 smaller ones. Successively finer divisions of time would bring the graph steadily closer to the smooth curve for a continuous variate. However, this is possible because the variate is not essentially discrete. In Figure 5.2, if y represented 'number of children per family' for all mothers in a city or 'number of previous convictions' for all persons recently convicted of motoring offences, no finer division of the y-scale would be meaningful and the step-function would be an intrinsic feature of the population.

Real data relating to any continuous variate are, strictly speaking, necessarily grouped into discrete form. Weight is not measured exactly but to the nearest 1 kg, nearest 10 kg, nearest 1 μg, etc. The Gopain data were coarsely grouped in units of 1 day, but we can conceive of them being recorded to the nearest minute. Even coarse grouping does not seriously disturb the practical validity of the basic methods of analysis for continuous variates.

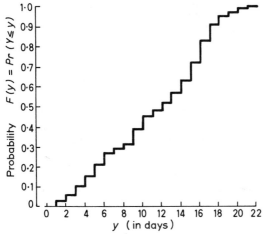

Figure 5.2. A possible cumulative distribution function for number of days between administration of Gopain and onset of jaundice.

5.3* **Probability density**

Elementary statistical texts commonly introduce continuous variates by way of frequency functions. However the probabilities required for inferences must then be obtained by integration; the equivalent approach of going directly to the cumulative distribution function avoids a step that is difficult for those who are unfamiliar with integral calculus. Some readers may already have met frequency functions and frequency distributions; for them, the present section may help in the connection of ideas. Others may omit the section.

The rate of increase of $F(y)$ relative to y, which is the slope of the $F(y)$ curve at a specified value of y or the differential coefficient of $F(y)$ with respect to y, is the average increase in probability corresponding to unit increase in y. Thus the rate of increase is the average 'density' of probability at y. When $F(y)$ is a smooth curve, we write

$$\mathrm{d}F(y)/\mathrm{d}y = f(y);$$

$f(y)$ is the *probability density function* of y, known for short as the 'p.d.f.' of y and also as the *frequency function*.

From elementary consideration of relative frequencies, for any a, b with $a < b$,

$$Pr(a < Y \leqslant b) = Pr(Y \leqslant b) - Pr(Y \leqslant a)$$
$$= F(b) - F(a).$$

This is merely a symbolic statement of the fact that all values of y that exceed a but are less than or equal to b can be regarded as all values less than or equal to b reduced by all those that are also less than or equal to a. From elementary mathematics, this can also be written

$$Pr(a < Y \leqslant b) = \int_a^b f(y)\mathrm{d}y.$$

Corresponding to the distribution function in Figure 5.1, we can plot the p.d.f. as in Figure 5.3, and see that the required probability of a weight lying between a and b is the shaded area beneath the curve. Clearly if A, B are respectively the lowest and the highest possible values for y (the smallest and the greatest weight for an adult male; 0 and the longest time to appearance of jaundice), then

$$\int_a^b f(y)\mathrm{d}y = F(B) - F(A) = 1.0.$$

In practice, A and B are not very easily specified: we cannot readily say what is the smallest possible weight for a man. I have implied earlier that we *know* $A = 40$, $B = 120$, but of course in reality we have no such exact knowledge: perhaps $A = 43$ or $A = 38$ or $A = 27$. Consequently the limits are very often taken as infinite, so that we write

$$\int_{-\infty}^{\infty} f(y)\mathrm{d}y = 1.0.$$

This includes the earlier possibility, because $f(y)$ can be defined as 0 for $y \leqslant A$ or $y > B$, so corresponding to something that should be obvious from Figure 5.1, namely

$$F(y) = 0 \quad \text{if} \quad y \leqslant A$$
$$F(y) = 1 \quad \text{if} \quad y > B.$$

In the general presentation of statistics, one usually assumes the limits infinite unless there is special reason to state the contrary. You will perhaps want to question the appearance of '$-\infty$', since even a finite negative value is meaningless for a human weight or an interval before jaundice appears. We could instead write '0' for the lower limit. However, some variates will permit negative values, for example change in body temperature between 12.00 and 18.00 hours, difference in birth weight between first and second calves from the same cow. No harm is done by taking the extreme limits every time with the condition that $f(y) = 0$ over certain ranges of y.

The statement about the total integral being 1.0 is equivalent to

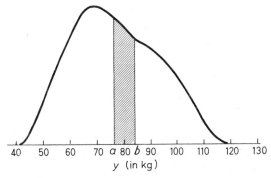

Figure 5.3.   Probability density function roughly corresponding to Figure 5.1. Total area below curve = 1.0; Area shaded = $Pr(a < Y \leqslant b)$.

Equation [2.I] in Section 2.7. It is mathematical shorthand for 'If all possible results are taken into consideration, the probability is 1.0 that one of them will happen'.

5.4 Parameters and statistics

The distinction between a parameter and a statistic was made in Section 2.6. A parameter is a property of a population, a statistic is a quantity calculated from a sample, and therefore taking different values for different samples from the same population. A statistic summarizes some aspect of the information provided by a sample, usually in order to estimate the numerical value of a parameter, or to make a probability statement (such as a statement of statistical significance) about the parameter.

5.5 Population and sample means

A very important parameter of a population is the *population mean*. For a discrete variate, y, for which the possible values are $0, 1, 2, 3, \ldots$, this mean is μ, defined by

$$\mu = 0 \times Pr(y = 0) + 1 \times Pr(y = 1) + 2 \times Pr(y = 2) + \ldots .$$

Each value is multiplied by the limiting relative frequency of its occurrence in the population. For example, if in a population of plants 30% have 4 leaves, 40% have 5 leaves, 25% have 6 leaves, and 5% have 8 leaves, then

$$\mu = 4 \times 0.30 + 5 \times 0.40 + 6 \times 0.25 + 7 \times 0.00 + 8 \times 0.05$$
$$= 5.10$$

More concisely, the general formula is

$$\mu = \sum r \, Pr(y = r) \qquad\qquad [5.\text{IV}]$$

where Σ implies summation over all possible values of y (cf. Equation [3.III]).

For a continuous variate, the summation must be replaced by the analogous integration. If you are not familiar with the terminology and symbolism of elementary integral calculus, you need not worry about understanding details. The mean is

$$\mu = \int_{-\infty}^{\infty} y f(y) \mathrm{d}y$$

where $f(y)$ is the probability density function (Section 5.3). For either kind of variate, the population mean is the same as the expectation of y (see Section 5.8)

$$\mu = E(y). \qquad [5.V]$$

Except in a few special circumstances, the population mean is unknown because the underlying probabilities cannot be known. We are much more concerned with data from the sample. The *sample mean* for a set of n observations is the statistic

$$\bar{y} = \left(\sum_{i=1}^{n} y_i \right) \Big/ n \qquad [5.VI]$$

where $y_1, y_2, \ldots, y_n$ are the symbols for the n observations; the name of the statistic is read 'y-bar'. Of course we have already used this formula at the foot of Table 1.1, and it is certainly familiar to you even if you have not expressed it this way.

5.6 Estimators

The statistic $\bar{y}$ is said to be an *estimator* of the parameter μ. Is this a statement of the obvious? Life is not always quite so simple, as Section 5.7 illustrates. One important feature is that if we take larger and larger samples, so that n steadily increases, $\bar{y}$ is almost certain to get closer and closer to μ, a behaviour similar to that illustrated in Table 2.1. This property of an estimator is known as *consistency*. Not only is $\bar{y}$ a consistent estimator, it is also *unbiased* whatever the size of sample. That is to say, if we could look at every possible sample of size n, and calculate $\bar{y}$ for each, the average of all the $\bar{y}$ would be exactly μ. This may seem so obvious as not to deserve mention: logically it requires formal proof, but I shall not inflict this on the reader.

5.7 Variance

Another characteristic of a distribution, very important to the interpretation of observations, is the variability among individual values. If the times to appearance of jaundice in series D had been less markedly unequal, we should scarcely need statistical science to help us interpret them! But suppose they had been

$$11, 13, 12, 14, 11, 12, 11$$

or

$$1, 2, 43, 1, 1, 3, 33.$$

Both series also have $\bar{y} = 12$; evidently the first is much less variable and the second much more variable than D. Many ways of measuring variability can be suggested; for example, the 7 observations had a *range* of 17 (= 20 − 3) from largest to smallest, as compared with 3 and 42 for the series I have just quoted. Although *sample range* can be found in this way, *population range* is open to practical and theoretical objections; the concept of the longest possible interval before jaundice appears (100 days?, 5000 days?), like the smallest or greatest possible weight for a man (Section 5.3), has conceptual difficulties.

The most used measure of variability is the *variance*. The parameter *population variance*, denoted by σ^2, is the mean value of squared deviations from μ. In the notation of Section 5.5, for a discrete variate

$$\sigma^2 = \sum (r - \mu)^2 \times Pr(y = r). \qquad [5.\text{VII}]$$

You will understand better, perhaps, by looking at variance for the number of leaves per plant in the example in Section 5.5:

$$\sigma^2 = (4 - 5.1)^2 \times 0.30 + (5 - 5.1)^2 \times 0.40 + (6 - 5.1)^2 \times 0.25$$
$$+ (7 - 5.1)^2 \times 0.00 + (8 - 5.1)^2 \times 0.05$$
$$= 0.99.$$

For a continuous variate, $(y - \mu)^2$ must be averaged over the whole distribution (in place of averaging y for the mean):

$$\sigma^2 = \int_{-\infty}^{\infty} (y - \mu)^2 f(y) dy.$$

Again we need a statistic to use as an estimator of σ^2 from the sample observations. If

$$\sum_{1}^{n} (y_i - \mu)^2 / n$$

were a statistic, it could be calculated, and would be very suitable. Except for rare special circumstances in which the true mean, μ, is known, this cannot be calculated. Replacement of μ by $\bar{y}$ introduces a bias, but a simple modification adjusts for this; algebra that is simple but tedious, and that is presented in the solutions to Exercises 5.3–5.5, proves that

$$s^2 = \sum_{1}^{n} (y_i - \bar{y})^2 / (n - 1) \qquad [5.\text{VIII}]$$

is an unbiased estimator of σ^2, in the sense that (like $\bar{y}$ in Section 5.6) its expectation is exactly equal to the parameter being estimated. Because s^2 is calculated entirely from the sample (it does not use μ) it is a statistic and is termed the *sample variance*. Calculation of the sum of squares of deviations from the mean, the numerator of the right-hand side of Equation [5.VIII], is often made quicker by using the formula (see Exercise 5.3 with $d = 0$):

$$\sum_{1}^{n} (y_i - \bar{y})^2 = \sum_{1}^{n} y_i^2 - \left(\sum_{1}^{n} y_i \right)^2 \Big/ n. \qquad [5.IX]$$

The choice of method for arithmetic should depend upon convenience and the mechanical aids available. With small numerical values, especially the carefully chosen ones used for many examples in this book, almost all the arithmetic involved in Equation [5.VIII] can be done rapidly with pen and paper. With more extensive data, analysed by hand or with a calculator, Equation [5.IX] is usually quicker; some pocket calculators (see Section 10.3) incorporate programs that will do the whole computation with little more effort than entering the values of y. For reasons of numerical accuracy with large bodies of data, a computer more commonly operates with Equation [5.VIII] or with an alternative introduced in the solution to Exercise 5.3.

Note that since σ^2 and s^2 are obtained by adding multiples of squares of the basic observations, they are measured in 'squared' units. If the variate y represents height measured in cm, then the variance is measured in cm^2; if y is a weight in kg, then variance is measured in kg^2, a unit without direct physical interpretation (see Section 5.9).

5.8 Expectation

Section 5.6 referred to the concept of 'every possible sample of size n' from a population. This can be regarded as constituting a 'super-population'. For each member of the superpopulation, i.e. each possible sample, a value of $\bar{y}$ exists. By an extension of the ideas that underlie Section 3.5, the mean of $\bar{y}$ in its superpopulation is known as the expectation of $\bar{y}$, symbolized by $E(\bar{y})$. When we say that $\bar{y}$ is an unbiased estimator of μ, the population mean of y in the original population, we mean

$$E(\bar{y}) = \mu. \qquad [5.X]$$

An earlier result, Equation [5.V], can be regarded as the particular case of this for samples with $n = 1$.

The expectation function is not limited to $\bar{y}$. Suppose that u is any statistic: that is to say u represents a rule for making a calculation on values from any sample. Just as with $\bar{y}$, u has a value for each sample of the superpopulation, and $E(u)$ denotes the mean of u in that superpopulation. The variance of u, the mean value of squared deviations from the population mean, can now be defined as

$$Var(u) = E[\{u - E(u)\}^2].$$

The general '$Var(\ )$' notation is useful in discussion of any statistic derived from the original observations. For the observations themselves, where y plays the part of u, we have the shorter and special notation:

$$\sigma^2 = E[(y - \mu)^2]. \qquad [5.XI]$$

As indicated in Section 5.7, estimation of variance involves the sum of squares of deviations from $\bar{y}$, not μ. By a little algebraic manipulation (Exercise 5.5),

$$E[\Sigma(y_i - \bar{y})^2] = (n - 1)\sigma^2$$

can be proved. Hence with s^2 as before

$$\begin{aligned} E(s^2) &= E[\Sigma(y_i - \bar{y})^2/(n - 1)] \\ &= \sigma^2 \end{aligned} \qquad [5.XII]$$

meaning that s^2 is an unbiased estimator of σ^2. This follows because, if k is any numerical constant and u is any statistic,

$$E(ku) = kE(u); \qquad [5.XIII]$$

k may be taken as $1/(n - 1)$. A similarly important result for two statistics, u_1 and u_2, is

$$E(u_1 + u_2) = E(u_1) + E(u_2). \qquad [5.XIV]$$

These two statements are practically obvious: Equation [5.XIII] simply states that (for example) the mean value of 7.3 times a quantity is equal to 7.3 times the mean value of the quantity itself, and Equation [5.XIV] states that the mean value of the total of two quantities can be obtained by adding the separate means. Nevertheless, they are powerful aids to simplifying statistical formulae.

5.9 Standard deviation

The square root of the variance, which is σ, is called the population *standard deviation* (or SD); correspondingly, s is the sample standard deviation. Despite what you might guess, s is not an unbiased estimator of σ; the reasons are not obvious without troublesome algebra, but a simple numerical example could easily be constructed to illustrate the point. Both σ and s are measured in exactly the same units as the original measurements, that is to say in days for the Gopain records, in cm for the heights of a human population recorded in cm.

Variance and standard deviation are in one sense equivalent measures of variation, since either is easily calculated from the other. Both names are needed, because variance is usually the first to be calculated (and variances from different sources are easily combined) but SD is the more readily understood quantity to state in a report. Use SD to help describe your own data, but be aware of its derivation from variance.

A common practice is to express SD as a percentage of the mean; $100\,\sigma/\mu$ or $100\,s/\bar{y}$ is termed the *coefficient of variation*. Use of this quantity is sometimes actively misleading, often confusing or concealing practical issues, and rarely any gain over separate discussion of mean and SD. Avoid it unless you have very specific reasons for needing it.

EXERCISES

5.1 A species of insect is such that almost all males weigh between 100 mg and 200 mg, with 130–170 mg as the commonest, and almost all females weigh between 350 mg and 450 mg with 380–420 mg as the commonest. Sketch the general appearance of the distribution function for the whole population

    (a) if males and females are about equal in number;
and
    (b) if males form only about 20% of the population.

5.2 Sketch the form of distribution function that would give a qualitatively reasonable description for each of the following:

    (a) Ages of human beings in a 'stable' population, that is to say a population in which reproduction and death are so balanced as to ensure that the relative frequencies in different age groups remain constant from year to year;
    (b) Fractions of the sky obscured by cloud at noon on different days for a point in the central Sahara;

    (c) As (b), but for the Straits of Magellan;

    (d) As (b), but for the place in which you are reading this book?

    (e) Times spent by university students in any form of athletic activity during one week.

Exact answers are not possible, but you should have a reason for each broad feature of your curves.

(Exercises 5.3–5.5 contain important results in statistical algebra. They require more skill in manipulation of symbols than other parts of this book; some readers will prefer to ignore them or at most glance rapidly at them, but those who can follow the arguments will gain in understanding of later chapters.)

5.3 Prove that for any sample of n values of y_i and any quantity d

$$\sum_{i=1}^{n} (y_i - d)^2 = \sum_{i=1}^{n} (y_i - \bar{y})^2 + \left[\sum_{1}^{n} y_i - nd \right]^2 \Big/ n.$$

You will find that a helpful start is to write

$$y_i - d = (y_i - \bar{y}) + (\bar{y} - d),$$

and then to square and sum these expressions.

5.4 Suppose that the y_i in Exercise 5.3 come from an infinite population in which the mean and variance are μ and σ^2. Prove that

$$E(y_i^2) = \mu^2 + \sigma^2,$$

and that, if y_i and y_j are statistically independent

$$E(y_i y_j) = \mu^2.$$

Independence was explained in Section 3.1; one consequence is that knowledge of the deviation of y_i from expectation gives no information on the deviation of y_j, or

$$E[(y_i - \mu)(y_j - \mu)] = 0.$$

5.5 Use Exercise 5.4, and Equations [5.IX] and [5.XIII] to prove that, for a random sample of n independent values from the population in Excercise 5.4

$$E\left[\sum_{1}^{n} (y_i - \bar{y})^2 \right] = (n - 1)\sigma^2.$$

5.6 In Exercise 1.1, you found the numbers of men with arm spans of 156 cm, 157 cm, 158 cm, etc. By first forming cumulative totals of these $(2, 2 + 0, 2 + 0 + 0, 2 + 0 + 0 + 1,$ etc.) and then dividing by 150, find the proportions whose spans are 156 or less, 157 or less, 158 or less, etc. (i.e. 2/150, 2/150, 2/150, 3/150, ... 149/150, 150/150). Plot these proportions against the values 156, 157, 158, ... and draw a smooth curve through the points to represent an approximation to the cumulative distribution function. From your curve read approximations to the probability that a man has a span:

(a) 170 cm or less,
(b) greater than 180.5 cm,
(c) between 173 and 188 cm.

(No solution is given for this exercise, as the results obtained will depend upon the individual who draws the freehand curve).

6 Inference on means; the Normal distribution

6.1 Types of distribution function

Many natural distributions, including distributions of biological measurements, are approximately symmetric. They have distribution functions looking something like Figure 6.1. The symmetry consists in the upper right-hand section being superposable on the lower left-hand section if the diagram were to be pivoted at the centre point. There is no law that distribution functions must be symmetric. They can be as in Figures 6.2 and 6.3, of the type introduced in Exercise 5.1 and common for heterogeneous populations, like the extreme cases in Exercise 5.2, or more complicated.

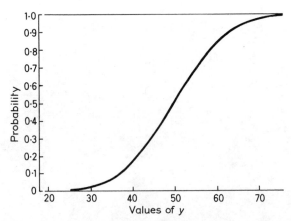

Figure 6.1.   A symmetric cumulative distribution function.

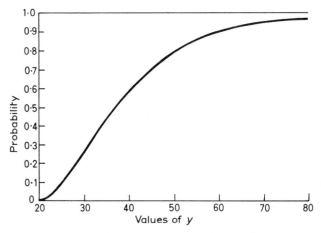

Figure 6.2. A positively skew cumulative distribution function (note that steepest slope comes early, and is followed by a slow flattening).

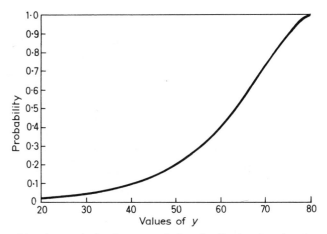

Figure 6.3. A negatively skew cumulative distribution function (note the slow rise to maximum slope and rapid flattening for large *y*).

6.2   Distribution of means

Section 5.8 mentioned how one distribution can be derived from another. As described there, if independent samples of *n* individuals are repeatedly selected from a population, a statistic calculated for a variate measured on members of the samples will have a new 'derived' distribution. Exercise 2.1 illustrated that if one takes a series of means of n (in that instance, $n = 5$) independently from a distribution, they are more tightly bunched than the single values. What I there illustrated for particular data is entirely general. We can talk about 'the distribution function for means of n' from a specified distribution, or simply about 'the distribution function of $\bar{y}$'. As Exercise 2.1 suggests, the behaviour for various n would be something like that in Figure 6.4.

This is the essential reason for scientific discussion of means rather than single observations. Why grow 10 plants instead of 1? Why study the rate of multiplication of 5 parallel cultures of bacteria instead of 1? Why do we wish to have several (7 in series D) patients recorded for time to appearance of jaundice instead of only 1? We do so to some extent to safeguard against accidents and gross mistakes, but primarily because of the phenomenon represented by Figure 6.4. With the notation and terminology already introduced, we have seen that

$$E(y) = \mu$$

and
$$E(\bar{y}) = \mu.$$

Hence, if we want to estimate the population mean, μ, either y or $\bar{y}$ can be used as an unbiased estimator – that is to say *either* a single value of y *or* a mean of n independent values from the population. Secondly, if

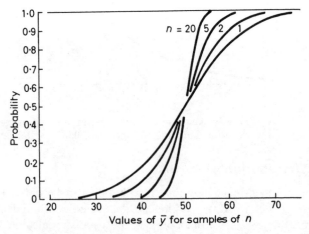

Figure 6.4.   Distribution function of Figure 6.1 repeated, together with distribution functions for means of 2, 5, and 10 from Figure 6.1.

for individual values of y the variance is

$$Var\,(y) = \sigma^2,$$

that for the distribution of $\bar{y}$ can be proved to be

$$Var\,(\bar{y}) = \sigma^2/n. \qquad [6.I]$$

This shows that $Var\,(\bar{y})$ can be made as small as we wish by taking n large enough: the dispersion of independent values of $\bar{y}$ about their expectation, μ, steadily decreases as n increases.

The formula for $Var\,(\bar{y})$ is one of the most important in the practice of statistics. *You must know and understand it*; Section 6.3 presents a proof, but you need not worry about the details of this.

6.3* **Probability density function**

Any reader who found Section 5.3 easier to understand than Section 5.2 will also prefer Section 6.2 to Section 6.1. To each of the distribution functions in Section 6.1 corresponds a probability density function (Section 5.3), and the symmetry of Figure 6.1 is perhaps more evident in the p.d.f. (Figure 6.5). The distributions in Figures 6.2 and 6.3 are commonly termed positively and negatively skewed, for reasons that Figures 6.6 and 6.7 make apparent. Figures 6.2 and 6.6 are typical of the many situations in which a measurement has a fairly well-defined lower limit but no clear upper limit; examples would be total weights of fruit from single apple trees in one year or times required by individual rats to find a route to the

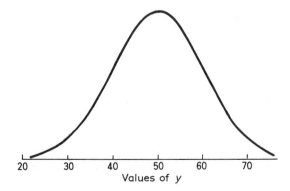

Figure 6.5. Symmetric probability density function (p.d.f. frequency function) corresponding to Figure 6.1.

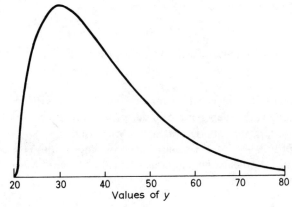

Figure 6.6. Positively skew probability density function corresponding to Figure 6.2.

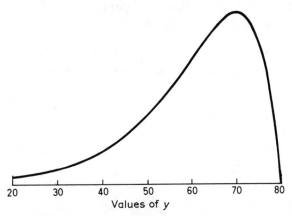

Figure 6.7. Negatively skew probability density function corresponding to Figure 6.3.

centre of a maze. Figures 6.3 and 6.7 are less often met, but represent the reverse state of affairs. Figure 6.8 illustrates a multimodal p.d.f. such as may arise when a population is a mixture of several heterogeneous components; a mixture does not always produce multimodality, nor is multimodality a guarantee of such an origin. You should sketch the bimodal p.d.f.'s corresponding to Exercise 5.1. Figure 6.9 shows the set of p.d.f. curves that corresponds with Figure 6.4; all have the same area between curve and base line, but the

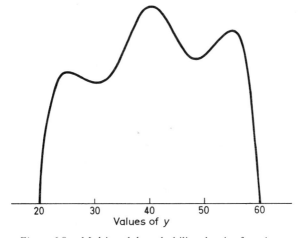

Figure 6.8.   Multimodal probability density function.

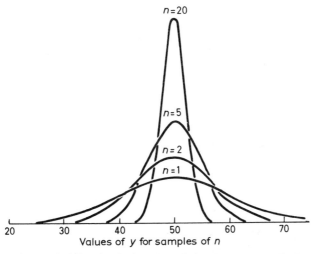

Figure 6.9.   Probability density function of Figure 6.5, and p.d.f.'s for means of 2, 5, and 10, corresponding to Figure 6.4.

larger the value of n the more is this area concentrated close to the mean.

6.4*   Variance of a mean

The truth of Equation [6.I] can be demonstrated by a few steps of algebra and reference to the independence of the n observations as well as to

$$E(\bar{y}) = E(y) = \mu.$$

We can write

$$
\begin{aligned}
Var\,(\bar{y}) &= E[\{\bar{y} - E(\bar{y})\}^2] \\
&= n^{-2} E[(n\bar{y} - n\mu)^2] \\
&= n^{-2} E[\{(y_1 - \mu) + (y_2 - \mu) + \ldots + (y_n - \mu)\}^2] \\
&= n^{-2} E[(y_1 - \mu)^2 + (y_2 - \mu)^2 + \ldots + (y_n - \mu)^2 \\
&\quad + 2(y_1 - \mu)(y_2 - \mu) + \ldots] \\
&= n^{-2} E[(y_1 - \mu)^2] + n^{-2} E[(y_2 - \mu)^2] + \ldots \\
&\quad + 2n^{-2} E[(y_1 - \mu)(y_2 - \mu)] + \ldots.
\end{aligned}
$$

But $y_1, y_2, \ldots$ are observations all having the same distribution, and therefore all $(y_i - \mu)^2$ have the same expectation. Similarly, all the $\frac{1}{2}n(n-1)$ expressions of the form $(y_i - \mu)(y_j - \mu)$ for $i \neq j$ have the same expectation. Hence

$$
\begin{aligned}
Var\,(\bar{y}) &= n^{-2} \cdot nE[(y_1 - \mu)^2] + n^{-2} \cdot \tfrac{1}{2}n(n-1)E[(y_1 - \mu)(y_2 - \mu)] \\
&= n^{-1}\sigma^2,
\end{aligned}
$$

because (i) the first expectation by definition is σ^2,

   (ii) independence of observations means that knowledge of the value of y_2 is unaffected by knowing y_1 and vice versa, so that, in finding the mean value of any expression involving both, one can first average over y_1 and then over y_2:

$$
\begin{aligned}
E[(y_1 - \mu)(y_2 - \mu)] &= E[\{E(y_1) - \mu\}(y_2 - \mu)] \\
&= E[(\mu - \mu)(y_2 - \mu)] = 0
\end{aligned}
$$

6.5 Standardized unit deviate

Starting from any mean of n independent observations (including $n = 1$ as a possibility), we can usefully transform to a *standardized unit deviate*. **Do not confuse with the standard deviation** (Section 5.9). We obtain a quantity unaffected by scales of measurement, which therefore has certain absolute properties that assist inference. Some people refer to what follows under the name of 'z-scores', but this name is not universally accepted. Other writers use the symbols 'u' and 'd'. I choose the notation here as the most consistent with general statistical practice, and define

$$t = \frac{\bar{y} - \mu}{\sqrt{(\sigma^2/n)}}. \qquad [6.II]$$

Like $\bar{y}$, t is a quantity derived from the original distribution of y, and it also possesses a distribution. The definition of t expresses $\bar{y}$ in standardized terms, first as a deviation from its mean and then rescaled in units based upon the SD of the distribution of $\bar{y}$. The first step ensures that t, like $(\bar{y} - \mu)$, has mean zero:

$$E(t) = 0,$$

and the rescaling can easily be shown to lead to

$$Var(t) = 1$$

(formal proof is trivial but unimportant here).

   This form of t is of restricted practical interest, because with genuine data μ and σ^2 are usually both unknown. Note however that, just as $\bar{y}$ has a probability distribution derived from that of the original y, so also t has its own distribution. The mean and the variance of t are simple and other important properties are described below. One merit of t is that it expresses the departure of $\bar{y}$ from its mean in a way that is independent of origin and of scale of measurement: if y relates to measurements of weights in a sample from a population, t will have the same numerical value whether the weighings are in mg or kg or ounces, and if y refers to temperatures t will be the same whether the temperature is measured in $^\circ$ C, $^\circ$ F, or K. Section 6.7 will illustrate how, if σ^2 were known and therefore μ the only unknown quantity, the distribution of t in conjunction with the known value of $\bar{y}$ can be used to make inferences about μ; Chapter 7 will then be concerned with overcoming the difficulty of not knowing σ^2 and maintaining the same essential logic with an estimate of σ^2.

6.6   Normal, or Gaussian, distribution

A further remarkable property of the standardized unit deviate is vitally important. Whatever the distribution (continuous or discrete) of individual values of y, apart from a few oddities unimportant to us, t as defined by Equation [6.II] has a distribution function that tends to a fixed form as the sample size, n, increases.

Proof involves advanced mathematics, and you need not even remember the form of the result:[†]

$$F(t) = \int_{-\infty}^{t} \frac{1}{\sqrt{(2\pi)}} \exp\left(-\tfrac{1}{2}u^2\right) du.$$

Moreover, for most initial distributions, approach to the limiting form is good even for moderately small n. The limiting form is known as the standardized *Normal distribution* (write as 'Normal', not 'normal', for the word is used in a special sense) or *Gaussian distribution* (referring to the mathematician Gauss).

This may seem almost too good to be true. In fact many biological measurements have distributions well approximated by the general Normal (Section 6.7) even in circumstances that cannot permit exact Normality. Methods of analysis of data based upon Normality will usually (not always) work well when means are under discussion. However even a small departure from Normality may have serious consequences for such properties of data as the *range* of a sample (the difference between the smallest and the largest value) or the expectation of the maximum that will be encountered in 30 observations.

6.7 Normal distribution function

The distribution function for the standardized Normal is like that in Figure 6.1, suitably scaled. Figure 6.10 shows more detail; from a carefully drawn version, values of t corresponding to specified values of $F(t)$ could be read. We need not worry about the complicated calculations, as standard tables exist. The symmetry ensures that $E(t)$ corresponds to a probability of $\tfrac{1}{2}$, or

$$F(0) = 0.5.$$

Other probabilities symmetrically placed relative to 0.5 correspond to equal and opposite values of t, as illustrated in Figure 6.10. For example

$$F(1.96) = 0.5 + 0.475 = 0.975,$$
$$F(-1.96) = 0.5 - 0.475 = 0.025,$$

and
$$F(1.00) = 0.841,$$
$$F(-1.00) = 0.159.$$

[†] In statistical and computing usage, 'exp' is often written to represent the exponential function; $\exp(x)$ is the same as e^x. In the integral, u is merely a dummy variable used for integration.

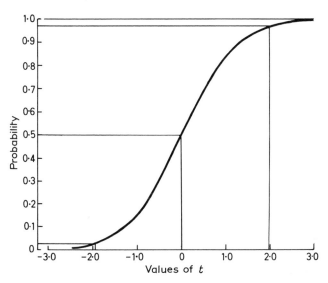

Figure 6.10.   Standardized Normal cumulative distribution function.

Statisticians use many special tables of numerical values. You are doubtless familiar with tables of logarithms, trigonometric sines, and other standard functions, even though you do not know how they were produced. Statistical tables are as easily used. Many tables of the standardized Normal distribution function exist; the most useful is not in the direct form but a table to show the probability that a calculated value of t will lie within a range A on either side of 0. We might define

$$G(A) = Pr(-A \leqslant t \leqslant A)$$
$$= Pr(t \leqslant A) - Pr(t < -A); \qquad [6.\text{III}]$$

all possible ways for t to lie between $-A$ and A can be regarded as all ways for t to be less than or equal to A reduced by those in which t is also less than $-A$. Hence

$$G(A) = F(A) - F(-A).$$

Table 6.1 provides a short selection of useful values; many statistical texts and books of tables give far more.

If we require the distribution function, we can use

$$F(A) = 1 - F(-A) = \tfrac{1}{2}[1 + G(A)].$$

Table 6.1 The function $G(A) = Pr(-A \leqslant t \leqslant A)$ (standardized Normal distribution)

A	0.0	0.5	1.0	1.28	1.5	1.64	1.96	2.0	2.5	2.58	3.0
$G(A)$	0.0	0.383	0.682	0.800	0.866	0.900	0.950	0.954	0.988	0.990	0.997

For example

$$F(1.0) = 1 - F(-1.0) = \tfrac{1}{2}(1 + 0.682)$$
$$= 0.841.$$

The p.d.f. for a Normal distribution looks similar to Figure 6.5. The standardized Normal distribution, with mean 0 and variance 1, is frequently referred to by the abbreviation $N(0, 1)$. It has a p.d.f. with height above the horizontal axis

$$f(y) = \frac{1}{\sqrt{(2\pi)}} \exp(-y^2/2).$$

The total area between the curve and the axis is 1.0. Table 6.1 corresponds with a central area such as that shaded in Figure. 6.11. This has been drawn to correspond roughly to $A = 1.64$, for which the shaded area is 0.90. More generally, the Normal distribution with mean μ and variance σ^2 is known as $N(\mu, \sigma^2)$; the ordinate is

$$f(y) = \frac{1}{\sigma\sqrt{(2\pi)}} \exp[-(y - \mu)^2/2\sigma^2].$$

Thus $(y - \mu)/\sigma$ has the distribution $N(0, 1)$.

6.8 Limits of error

Suppose that the Gopain data in Table 1.1 come from distributions such that the approach to Normality will be good even for samples as small as 7 or 5. What use can be made of Sections 6.6 and 6.7? For series D we had

$$\bar{y} = 12.0 \quad \text{with} \quad n = 7.$$

Forming t as defined in Equation [6.II] and using its properties as explained in Sections 6.6 and 6.7, we can assert that

$$t = (12.0 - \mu)/\sqrt{(\sigma^2/7)}$$

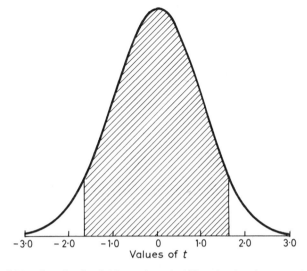

Figure 6.11. Standardized Normal probability density function (shaded area, with ordinates at $A = -1.64$, $A = 1.64$, gives a probability of 0.90).

will approximately follow the standardized Normal distribution. If we knew the value of σ^2, we could use the G function to make an inference about μ. In real life, σ^2 is rarely known. I delay discussion of how then to proceed until Chapter 7; the logic is well illustrated by a simpler specification in which we suppose that 'special circumstances' have allowed us to know

$$\sigma^2 = 28.0.$$

Hence

$$t = (12.0 - \mu)/\sqrt{4.0}$$
$$= (12.0 - \mu)/2.0.$$

By reference to Table 6.1, we know

$$Pr(-1.5 \leqslant t \leqslant 1.5) = 0.866.$$

The double inequality is satisfied by all values of μ between $12.0 - 1.5 \times 2.0$ and $12.0 + 1.5 \times 2.0$, or 9.0 and 15.0. Thus we can associate these limits to μ with the probability 0.866. In rather more than 6/7 of trials, if we proceed in this manner, we shall be correct in making an assertion of the type 'μ lies between 9.0 and 15.0'.

In statistical practice, the probability 0.95 is commonly chosen. We write

$$Pr[- 1.96 \leqslant (12.0 - \mu)/2.0 \leqslant 1.96] = 0.95.$$

The only values of μ for which the inequalities are true are those between μ_L and μ_U, where

$$\mu_L = 12.0 - 1.96 \times 2.0 = 8.1$$
$$\mu_U = 12.0 + 1.96 \times 2.0 = 15.9.$$

These are termed *fiducial limits* or *confidence limits* to μ at probability 0.95. We can assert that, unless a rare chance has occurred (probability $1 - 0.95 = 0.05$ or 1 in 20), the values in D come from a population whose mean lies between 8.1 and 15.9 days. If we want a still stronger assurance, we can use a larger probability and quote wider limits: probability 0.99 leads to the fiducial range 6.8 days to 17.2 days. If A is the value in Table 6.1 corresponding to the required probability, the limits can be expressed in a concise formula:

$$\mu_L = \bar{y} - A\sigma/\sqrt{n}, \quad \mu_U = y + A\sigma/\sqrt{n}. \qquad [6.IV]$$

Any frequent user of the method will remember the formula and so avoid the need to work through the whole argument every time.

6.9* Non-parametric methods

Despite what I said in Section 6.6, there are data for which methods of analysis based upon Normal and related distributions are unsuitable. This is particularly common for strongly subjective data, for example records relating to aesthetic, ethical, or sensory judgement. The data may consist merely of an order of preference ('D is more beautiful – or more painful – than G, which is more beautiful than C, . . .'), or of arbitrary grades on a conventionally numerical scale (as when severity of insect attack on plants is graded from 1 to 10). Even with more objective records, a distribution can be very obviously non-Normal, for example the annual consumption of alcohol by adults.

Statistical methods are available that avoid any assumption of Normality of any other fully-specified distribution. We have already used them in Section 4.2 for two significance tests applied to the Gopain data. Numerical records are easily reduced to the simpler gradings appropriate to purely comparative or categorical data (Section 5.2), and these or other non-parametric or distribution-free tests (the names are almost equivalent) can be applied. Many analogous tests exist, those known as Wilcoxon and Mann–Whitney being particularly popular. Estimation procedures are more troublesome but not impossible. Though I would not advise general adoption of these methods in biology, they may be especially appropriate to some types of work.

EXERCISES

6.1 The score, y, for a psychological test is known to have a variance of 225.0 in populations of 10 year old children of either sex. In a particular locality, randomly selected samples of 9 girls and 25 boys all aged 10 show mean scores of 86.0 and 84.0, respectively. Obtain fiducial limits to the population mean score for girls at probability 0.95 and at probability 0.99; find the corresponding limits for boys.

6.2 Under the conditions of Exercise 6.1, how many girls and how many boys should be tested in order that the limits at probability 0.99 shall be distant at most 2.0 on either side of the corresponding means of the observed y's?

6.3 For series D and series E of Table 1.1 (taken separately), evaluate the sum of squares of deviations from the mean, using each of the two expressions in Equation [5.IX] in turn. Repeat on each of the series of 7 values stated at the beginning of Section 5.7.

6.4 For the numerical values

$$y_1 = 1, \quad y_2 = 4, \quad y_3 = 5, \quad y_4 = -5$$

and using in turn the first two, the first three, and all four, find $\bar{y}$ and $\Sigma(y_i - \bar{y})^2$. Recalculate $\Sigma(y_i - \bar{y})^2$ by the alternative formula on the right-hand side of Equation [5.IX] and again by the alternative formula stated in the solution to Exercise 5.3.

6.5 If u_1, u_2 are any two observed values or combinations of observed values, independent of one another, and k is a numerical constant, you may assume the truth of Equations [5.XIII] and [5.XIV] and

$$Var(ku_1) = k^2 \, Var(u_1),$$
$$Var(u_1 + u_2) = Var(u_1) + Var(u_2).$$

Suppose $\bar{y}, \bar{z}$ to be means of two sets of independent observations, such that $E(\bar{y}) = E(\bar{z}) = \mu$, and suppose the variances of $\bar{y}, \bar{z}$ to be

H, J. Using the formula stated, prove that for any constant f

$$E[f\bar{y} + (1 - f)\bar{z}] = \mu$$
$$Var[f\bar{y} + (1 - f)\bar{z}] = f^2 H + (1 - f)^2 J.$$

By expanding expressions in brackets, verify that the last result can be written in the alternative form

$$(H + J)\left(f - \frac{J}{H + J}\right)^2 + \frac{HJ}{H + J}.$$

Using differential calculus or this formula, show that the variance of the weighted combination of $\bar{y}$, $\bar{z}$ is minimized by choosing

$$f = \frac{J}{H + J},$$

and state the minimum value.

6.6 The potency of a certain drug (relative to a standard drug) is estimated by an experiment on rats as 91.0, with variance 12.0, and by an independent experiment using mice as 94.0, with variance 6.0. There are theoretical reasons for believing the true potency to be the same in both species. Use Exercise 6.5 to find the combined estimate that has minimum variance.

7 Unknown variance; the *t*-distribution

7.1 Consequences of estimating variance

The logic of Chapter 6 is important; the methods can seldom be used because σ^2 is scarcely ever known. From n independent observed values of y, we can estimate σ^2 by

$$s^2 = \sum_{i=1}^{n} (y_i - \bar{y})^2/(n-1). \qquad [5.\text{VIII}]$$

This is unbiased and in some senses the best estimate that can be formed. However s^2 is not the same as σ^2, and what has been said about t is not exactly true if s^2 replaces σ^2. The divisor, here the number of observations minus one, plays an important part in the methods that follow. In further generalizations, s^2 is calculated as a modified sum of squares divided by a number that is not simply $(n-1)$; I shall illustrate this in Chapter 9, but for the present simply warn against any assumption that 'divide by $(n-1)$' is the universal rule. The appropriate divisor is known as the number of *degrees of freedom* (d.f.). Intuition suggests that when n is very large s^2 will almost certainly be close to σ^2. This is true; if the number of d.f. exceeds 100, one can safely use t as in Chapter 6. If the number of d.f. is smaller, substitution of s^2 for σ^2 in t as defined in Equation [6.II] broadens the distribution of values in consequence of the additional uncertainty introduced, and so allows higher probabilities for extreme values (cf. Table 7.1).

7.2 The *t*-distribution

If the distribution of individual observations is Normal, but the variance is unknown, inference based on $N(0, 1)$ is no longer possible.

A very simple change permits the same logic to be used. The deviate tabulated in Table 6.1 must be replaced by a deviate dependent upon the number of degrees of freedom attached to s^2. For each number of d.f., there is a distinct distribution function; the sequence of functions approaches more and more closely to $N(0, 1)$ as the d.f. become many. Table 7.1 generalizes Table 6.1, for five probabilities only. We now replace the definition in Equation [6.II] by

$$t = \frac{\bar{y} - \mu}{\sqrt{(s^2/n)}}, \qquad [7.I]$$

with s^2 being an estimate of variance from Equation [5.VIII] or an analogous formula. If we need to emphasize that there are f degrees of freedom, we write t_f instead of simply t. Corresponding to Equation [6.III], we define

$$G_f(A) = Pr(-A \leqslant t_f \leqslant A). \qquad [7.II]$$

Table 7.1 shows the values of A corresponding to $G_f(A) = 0.50, 0.80,$ 0.90, 0.95, 0.99 and for various values of f. The corresponding distribution function for the t-distribution is (as in Section 6.7)

$$F_f(A) = \tfrac{1}{2}[1 + G_f(A)].$$

The line headed 'Limit' can be regarded as relating to an infinite

Table 7.1 Values of A in Equation [7.II] for important probabilities

Degrees of freedom f	Probabilities, $G_f(A)$				
	0.50	0.80	0.90	0.95	0.99
1	1.00	3.08	6.31	12.7	63.7
2	0.82	1.89	2.92	4.30	9.92
3	0.76	1.64	2.35	3.18	5.84
4	0.74	1.53	2.13	2.78	4.60
5	0.73	1.48	2.02	2.57	4.03
6	0.72	1.44	1.94	2.45	3.71
8	0.71	1.40	1.86	2.31	3.36
10	0.70	1.37	1.81	2.23	3.17
20	0.69	1.32	1.72	2.09	2.84
40	0.68	1.30	1.68	2.02	2.70
Limit	0.67	1.28	1.64	1.96	2.58

(Note that four of the values from the final line of this table have already occurred with the same meaning in Table 6.1.)

number of degrees of freedom, under which condition s^2 must be equal to σ^2; on that line appear the values corresponding to the same probabilities in Table 6.1. Entries corresponding to other probabilities can be calculated, and tables much more extensive than Table 7.1 are available. When σ^2 is unknown and the number of d.f. is finite, the entry in Table 6.1 must be replaced by the corresponding one from Table 7.1 and the same logic used with it. Some authors do not like to use the symbol 't' for the standardized unit deviate or Normal deviate as in Chapter 6, but reserve it for the definition in Equation [7.I] that involves s^2 instead of σ^2. I deliberately use the same symbol, because Equation [6.II] is merely the particular case of Equation [7.I] applicable when s^2 has unlimited d.f. For a sample of n observations, $Var\,(\bar{y})$ is *always* σ^2/n, estimated by s^2/n. The number of d.f. for s^2 depends on what information we have for estimating σ^2; I emphasize again that we are currently looking at a problem in which the number of d.f. is $(n - 1)$, but it can be smaller or much greater in other problems.

7.3 Numerical examples

For series D of the Gopain data, Exercise 6.3 computed

$$\sum (y_i - \bar{y})^2 = 210;$$

this has 6 d.f., so leading to

$$s^2 = 210/6 = 35.0$$

(a little larger than the $\sigma^2 = 28.0$ assumed in Section 6.8). Hence

$$s^2/n = 5.0$$

and

$$t_6 = \frac{12.0 - \mu}{\sqrt{5.0}}.$$

Note the indication of the d.f. for t; it is wise to show this when there may be any uncertainty, but often the number need not be explicitly stated.

The limits for μ at probability 0.95 require the deviate $A = 2.45$, taken from Table 7.1 with $f = 6$. In other respects, the logic leading to Equation [6.IV] is unaltered, and

$$\mu_L = 12.0 - 2.45 \times \sqrt{5.0} = 6.5,$$
$$\mu_U = 12.0 + 2.45 \times \sqrt{5.0} = 17.5.$$

The limits are much wider than in Section 6.8, in part because s^2 chances to be greater than σ^2 and in part because the appropriate value of A has had to be increased from 1.96 to 2.45. Similarly for series E

$$s^2 = 50/4 = 12.5,$$

and the limits are (using $f = 4$, $A = 2.78$)

$$\mu_L = 6.0 - 2.78\sqrt{2.5} = 1.6,$$
$$\mu_U = 6.0 + 2.78\sqrt{2.5} = 10.4.$$

Note how small μ_L is. Had we calculated limits at probability 0.99, μ_L would have been negative. Obviously this indicates that something is wrong, for we are discussing a number of days, a variate that cannot take negative values. The explanation is that we are over-optimistic in applying a Normal or t-distribution to a small sample in which values of y are necessarily positive yet small and very variable. With a large enough n,

$$t = \frac{\bar{y} - \mu}{\sqrt{(\sigma^2/n)}}$$

will certainly tend to behave as $N(0, 1)$. Replacement of σ^2 by s^2 based on f degrees of freedom will give a statistic that conforms more and more closely to the distribution of t_f as n increases (irrespective of whether $f = n - 1$ or not). We cannot expect the approximation to work well for small n and extreme probabilities. You may safely use the method with 20 or more observations, you should be a little cautious with 10, and with fewer you should seek advice from someone with more experience of statistics.

7.4 Distributions in biology

There is no theoretical reason why the distribution of a biological measurement should be 'Normal'; the initial capital for this word is intended to remind you that it is not the opposite of 'abnormal'. There are reasons for expecting many measurements to have distributions that are approximately Normal. This can rarely be exact, because a true Normal distribution has 'tails' that stretch to infinity in either direction; expressed more simply, this means that whatever the values of μ and σ^2 may be there is a non-zero probability that an observation will exceed 1000.0 or even 100 000.0 and a non-zero probability that an observation will be less than 0.0 or even less than $-$ 10 000.0. If we are discussing weights of infants measured in kg, barometric pressures in mm, or intervals between Gopain and jaundice in days, these extremes are impossible, not merely improbable. Nevertheless, a measurement such as height of a plant, wool production of a sheep, or weight of a seed may be the resultant of a large number of small genetic and environmental effects, each affected by chance, and this can in part explain approximate Normality. Whatever the reason, many such types of measurement can be shown empirically to have approximately Normal distributions, and of course if this is true for individual values the trend to Normality of distribution of means (Section 6.6) is rapid.

The Normal distribution is of tremendous importance for reasons discussed in Section 6.6 and in the preceding paragraph. It is not universal. Some measurements have distributions that are so unsymmetric (or 'skew'), or so restricted by a lower limit at zero and no clear upper limit, that approximation by a Normal distribution cannot be satisfactory. An example is the daily consumption of alcohol by human adults: zero for many, a moderate amount for a great many more, but a few heavy drinkers consuming several times as much as the mean for the population. Measures of insect or bacterial infestation of individual plants may show similar distributions (cf. Figures 6.2, 6.6), as may lengths of life for an animal species that has a high mortality in infancy but the potentiality of living many years. Statisticians often *transform* such data, for example by basing their calculations on the logarithms (or the square roots or the reciprocals) of the original numerical values because the transformed values conform more satisfactorily to a Normal distribution. Although such transformations can be exploited successfully to assist statistical analysis and the interpretation of data, you will be wise to seek advice from a statistician before attempting this for yourself.

Throughout this book, the mean is regarded as the most interesting characteristic of a distribution, and the variance is considered only in so far as it relates to the precision of the mean and related inferential arguments. Some biological problems bring variance to the fore as the primary parameter for study; for example, in quantitative genetics different variance parameters need to be estimated in order to assess hereditary influences from various sources. These are matters of much greater difficulty.

7.5 Standard error

It is usual to refer to $\sqrt{(\sigma^2/n)}$ or $\sqrt{(s^2/n)}$ as the *standard error* (SE) of $\bar{y}$, and to write, for example,

$$\text{Estimated mean for } D = 12.0 \pm 2.2$$

where $2.2 \, (= \sqrt{5.0})$ is the estimated SE with 6 d.f. When you meet this symbolism, remember that some scientific writers use the 'plus-or-minus' symbol, $\pm$, to prefix the standard deviation (SD) instead of the SE; the SE involves dividing the corresponding SD by $\sqrt{n}$, and so the numerical magnitudes can be very different. A SD refers to the distribution of individual values, whereas a SE refers to the uncertainties associated with the estimate of a mean (or possibly of some other parameter). You will sometimes encounter a publication in which there is great difficulty in discovering whether '± 0.136' is intended as SE or SD: to leave this ambiguity is bad style, but unfortunately some people write carelessly. More rarely today, but still occasionally by physicists, $\pm$ is used to refer to a quantity called the 'probable error' which for excellent reasons ought to be abandoned by all scientists. Another unfortunate usage is that of employing the symbol in a compressed representation of upper and lower limits such as those of Equation [6.IV] and in Section 7.3; this should be avoided, and the two formulae for limits written separately, in order to avoid confusion.

In anything that *you* write, always make very clear whether you are referring to the SE of a specified mean or to the SD: the two are identical only for a 'mean' of one observation.

EXERCISES

7.1 A perfectly balanced cube has its six faces marked $1, -2, -2, 3, 3, 3$. It is thrown so that a random face is uppermost and the score, y, is recorded. Using Equations [5.IV] and [5.VII], prove that $E(y) = 1.0$ and $Var(y) = 5.0$.

7.2 Under the conditions of Exercise 7.1, two independent throws are made, giving scores y_1, y_2. Define $x = y_1 + y_2$. Prepare a table of 3 rows and 3 columns to show the possible combinations of values of y_1, y_2, the value of x corresponding to each combination, and the probability for each x. Prove that x takes the values $-4, -1, 1, 2, 4, 6$ with probabilities $4/36, 4/36, 12/36, 1/36, 6/36, 9/36$, respectively. Hence verify that

$$E(x) = E(y_1) + E(y_2) = 2 \times E(y) = 2.0$$
$$Var(x) = Var(y_1) + Var(y_2) = 2 \times Var(y) = 10.0.$$

7.3 For the two independent throws in Exercise 7.1, also define $v = y_1 - y_2$. Prepare a similar 3×3 table for v, find the probabilities for its seven possible values, and obtain $E(v)$, $Var(v)$. Hence infer how $E(v)$, $Var(v)$ are related to $E(y)$, $Var(y)$.

7.4 A random sample of 20 adult male animals of a certain species has a mean weight of 359.4 g. The estimated variance per animal, calculated from the sum of squares of deviations, is 500.0 g^2; the unit for variance is 'grammes squared', because it is based on squares of weights. Find the standard error of the mean. Construct a diagram that shows, in a visually effective manner, which values of the population mean (μ) are plausible, i.e. those values of μ from which 359.4 differs by an amount that does not correspond with an extreme probability. As an extension of Table 7.1, you may note that, for a probability 0.95, with 18, 19, 20 degrees of freedom the critical value of t is 2.101, 2.093, 2.086.

7.5 A biochemist requires 100 μg of a substance that can be isolated only from a certain species of plant. Experience has shown that on average a single plant yields 21 μg, but plants have a SD of 6 μg. The biochemist hopes that 5 plants will suffice. Describe the steps necessary for finding the probability that the total yield of 5 plants is at least 100 μg, and use Table 6.1 to gain some idea of this probability. You will probably find it easier to work in terms of mean yield per plant. Would 6 plants be much better than 5?

7.6 Suppose that in Exercise 4.13 a sample of 985 cells had been found to contain 220 Q-cells. The binomial probability calculation is intolerably laborious. Examine the null hypothesis by a χ^2 test. As an alternative, define for every cell a quantity y that takes the value 1 for a Q-cell, 0 otherwise. On the null hypothesis, the expectation of y is 0.25. Why? Analyse the values of y as though they were Normally distributed (they certainly are not!), and again examine the null hypothesis in the light of your analysis.

8 Design of experiments

8.1 Paired comparisons

In earlier chapters, I have discussed a very simple experiment on two treatments. In many practical situations, the subjects or materials fall naturally into groups, or can be organized as groups. For example:

(i) Rats from the same litter may be more alike in liability to tumours than rats from different litters, and two anti-epileptic drugs might be compared for risks of carcinogenesis by allocating each to one member of several pairs of litter-mates;

(ii) The potency of an antibiotic may be measured in terms of the extent to which it inhibits growth of a suitable bacterial culture on a plate of agar. Plates may differ in inherent capacity for growth, but two or more doses can be compared by applying each to a point on the same plate, repeating on several plates, and measuring the subsequent zones of inhibition of growth;

(iii) Strains A, B of a plant virus have been compared by inoculating left and right sides of a leaf with different strains (the technique will break down if and when two foci of infection begin to interact);

(iv) The durability of two types of nail varnish might be compared by inducing a sample of women to have type A on one hand, type B on the other. An additional precaution would be to have each type on equal numbers of right and left hands, so as to avoid any bias because the right hand tends to be worked harder;

(v) Alternative diets, A and B, for cattle have been compared on identical-twin calves;

(vi) Study of taste preferences in foodstuffs will generally be more satisfactory if each subject tries both 'brand A' and 'brand B' than if each subject tries only one and expresses his view on an arbitrary scale.

Such procedures eliminate variability between groups or pairs. The assessment of relative merit of two 'treatments' is unaffected by variations from one litter to another, different sensitivities to inoculation that may characterize different leaves, the fact that some women may care for their hands and use them less roughly than others, genetic differences in nutritional requirements of cattle, and so on.

In some circumstances, interpretation of results needs caution. For example, identical twins are an unusual phenomenon in cattle and man, and in many species of animal they are practically unknown: can one be confident that an advantage for diet A relative to diet B found in these atypical animals will be representative of what happens with more normal members of the species? Such a question cannot be answered by appeal to statistical theory. Is it right to assume that the effect of one dose of an antibiotic on a bacterial culture is unaffected by other doses or other antibiotics applied at different places on the plate? Is the normal activity of a woman unaffected by her knowledge that she is currently testing two types of nail varnish? In testing the flavours of cans of soup, what steps should be taken to ensure compatability of conditions, to guard against cues from sight and smell, and to eliminate any residual effect of the previous can on assessment of that under test?

8.2 Statistical analysis of paired comparisons

When only two treatments are involved, statistical analysis is easily put into essentially the same form as that illustrated in Section 7.3. The important step is to eliminate differences *between* pairs, since the experiment has been designed to balance these: because A and B are included in each pair, evaluation of any difference between A and B must not be affected by the fact that one litter of rats is much more sensitive to carcinogens than another, that Miss X ruins her nail varnish rapidly because of her occupation whereas Miss Y's work is much less damaging, that one pair of calves has the genetic capacity for rapid growth on any reasonable diet whereas another pair has not. For an experiment analogous to any of those described, we define y_i as a measure of the difference between A and B for pair i. Thus y_i might be a difference on plate i between growth inhibition for antibiotic A and inhibition for antibiotic B, or a difference for twin pair i between the weight increase for the calf fed on A and the weight increase for the calf on B over a 3-month-period. The difference is always taken in the same direction, say $(A - B)$. We then regard the n values of y_i exactly as though they were n observations in their own right. The method of Section 7.3 can be used to estimate the mean difference between A and B (i.e. μ) by $\bar{y}$, to enquire whether the hypothesis $\mu = 0$ is plausible, and to assign lower and upper limits μ_L, μ_U. Apart from the initial step of finding the n differences within pairs, the calculations are of exactly the same form.

8.3 Randomized blocks

Scientific questions often call for simultaneous comparisons among three or more treatments, for reasons indicated in Section 9.2. One treatment may be regarded as a *control*, to establish a base line for evaluation of others; such a control can be a zero level of some material that the experiment is intended to test, or a standard practice included in order to see whether alternatives represent improvements. In other circumstances, no one treatment is singled out as a control and all comparisons are seen as equally interesting.

The set of rules and constraints used to determine which treatment or combination of treatments shall be allocated to each subject or other experimental units is termed the *design* of the experiment. This statement, possibly difficult to comprehend at first reading, is best explained by reference to various examples. For obvious reasons, the experiment described in Section 1.4 is said to have a *completely randomized* design. The experiments outlined in Section 8.1 are *paired comparisons* or *randomized pairs*, a design that generalizes easily to *randomized blocks* for use when there are more than two treatments. Suppose five treatments (anaesthetics, diets, varieties of barley, etc.) are to be compared simultaneously. Find (or construct) *blocks* of 5 units as homogeneous as is practicable – 5 mice from the same litter, 5 adjacent plots of land in the same field – and assign treatments at random within each block in such a way that each treatment appears once in each block. Thus 5 diets A, B, C, D, E might be tested using any number of litters of 5 mice. For each litter, the first mouse would be allotted one of the 5 treatments at random, the second mouse one of the remaining 4, and so on. For example:

Litter

I	B,	D,	A,	E,	C
II	E,	C,	D,	B,	A
III	D,	E,	A,	B,	C
IV	D,	A,	C,	E,	B
V	A,	B,	D,	C,	E
VI	C,	E,	A,	B,	D
VII	C,	E,	D,	B,	A

⋮

You should regard an element of randomization as essential to any design, at least until you have considered most carefully the perils of omitting it. The statistical analysis of randomized blocks, a generalization of that for two treatments, involves an important technique known as *analysis of variance*, which I illustrate in Section 9.9.

8.4 Latin squares

Randomized blocks are easily constructed for any number of treatments. There are more complicated possibilities. The measurements to be made on animals that have received treatment A or B or C or D may require long and tedious analysis by one operator, perhaps dissection and careful measurement of liver cells. Work is to be shared between 4 operators p, q, r, s. These might use 4 litters of 4 mice:

Operator

Litter	p	q	r	s
I	B	D	C	A
II	A	C	D	B
III	C	A	B	D
IV	D	B	A	C

Note that each treatment occurs once in each litter, and also once with each operator so as to balance any differences in the techniques of the operators. Can you suggest how an analogous 5 × 5 square might be used so as to test 5 nail varnishes on 5 subjects? Or even on one subject by using her fingers on several successive occasions?

This arrangement, with each letter occurring once in each row and once in each column, is known as a 4 × 4 *Latin square*. Analogous $k \times k$ squares can be formed for any integer k. In effect, they establish two systems of blocks simultaneously. They are widely useful, especially (but by no means only) for control of positional effects. Thus A, B, C, D might represent four different varieties of apple and the diagram above could show relative positions of 16 trees in an orchard. Differences in soil fertility, drainage, etc., from north to south and from east to west are balanced, and when a correct analysis is made the standard error of a difference between any two varieties is likely to be smaller than if the design had been in randomized blocks or without any block constraints. In accordance with the principles of randomization, a 4 × 4 Latin square for use in an experiment ought to be chosen at random from 576 possible squares of this size. There are simple ways of doing this.

8.5 Some strange numbers

You should not need many minutes to satisfy yourself that there are only 2 different 2 × 2 Latin squares for the letters A, B, and only 12 squares of size 3 × 3 for the letters A, B, C. There is no simple formula for the number of squares of size k, but by ingenious tricks the answer has been found up to $k = 7$. Although the numbers have no practical importance, I think them sufficiently interesting to be worth listing:

4×4:　576
5×5:　161 280
6×6:　812 851 200
7×7:　61 479 419 904 000
8×8:　1.08776×10^{20}
9×9　5.52475×10^{27}

8.6 Graeco-Latin squares

In the example of litters and operators described for Latin squares, suppose that an operator can complete only one animal per day and that his standards may change from day to day (e.g. he may become more skilful with practice). The job must be done on 4 days, which we name $\alpha, \beta, \gamma, \delta$. Suppose that the previous specification is modified to:

	Operator			
Litter	p	q	r	s
I	Bγ	Dδ	Cα	Aβ
II	Aδ	Cγ	Dβ	Bα
III	Cβ	Aα	Bδ	Dγ
IV	Dα	Bβ	Aγ	Cδ

The treatments A, B, C, D are now also balanced over days, each occurring once with each of the Greek letters. Moreover, days are balanced over litters, so that consistency of day-to-day differences can be examined without disturbance from litter differences: in fact, the Greek letters also have the Latin square property of 'once in each row, once in each column'.

This design is a *Graeco-Latin square*. Suppose the Latin square had been only slightly different:

$$
\begin{array}{cccc}
B & D & C & A \\
A & C & B & D \\
C & A & D & B \\
D & B & A & C
\end{array}
$$

For this, no Graeco arrangement exists. An early speculation by mathematicians that no 6×6 Latin square can be extended to a Graeco-Latin required 150 years before a proof was found. After a further 50 years, the existence of some Graeco-Latin squares was proved for every size except 2×2 and 6×6. Except for those of size 3×3, relatively few Latin squares of any size have associated Graeco arrangements, and designs must be carefully chosen if Graeco properties are wanted.

8.7 Residual effects

The last square mentioned has another interesting use. Suppose the four diets A, B, C, D are to be supplied successively to an animal, and after each some measure of dose is recorded. The design

	Animal			
Period	1	2	3	4
I	B	D	C	A
II	A	C	B	D
III	C	A	D	B
IV	D	B	A	C

provides a safeguard against the possibility that the growth of an animal in any period is affected not only by its diet during that period but also by residual influence of the diet in the previous period. Each letter occurs once in Period I and once *preceded* by every other letter: thus A precedes C for animal 1, D precedes C for animal 2, and B precedes C for animal 4. Clearly C cannot precede itself. This again gives a special balance that enables an analysis to be performed in which residual effects of diets are eliminated or estimated separately. The design I have shown is but one example from a large family of related designs for various numbers of treatments.

8.8* Incomplete blocks

Often the number of experimental units that can be used for a block is fixed by circumstances outside the control of an investigator; identical twin cattle can be found but not triplets; a bilateral symmetry of most animals and of many plant leaves can be used to give blocks of two; cars have 4 wheels; a nutrient plate for microbiological work may accommodate 4 or perhaps 6 independent bacterial inoculations, but not more; litters of mice containing 4 or 5 females may be easily obtained, but sets of 8 or 9 female litter-mates are rare. On the other hand, limits to the number of treatments to be studied are set only by the ingenuity of the investigator. How are we to study, say, 11 treatments if our maximum block size is 6?

A number of valuable *Balanced Incomplete Block designs* have been found. The properties can be illustrated by the following arrangement of 13 treatments in blocks of 4:

Block	Treatments
I	A, B, C, J
II	D, E, F, J
III	G, H, I, J
IV	A, D, G, K
V	B, E, H, K
VI	C, F, I, K
VII	A, E, I, L
VIII	B, F, G, L
IX	C, D, H, L
X	A, F, H, M
XI	B, D, I, M
XII	C, E, G, M
XIII	J, K, L, M

Note that each of the 13 letters (representing treatments) occurs four times. Note also that every pair of letters (out of the $13 \times 12/2 \times 1$ possible pairs among 13) occurs in exactly one block: for example, B and H occur in Block V but no other block contains both. These two properties define balanced incomplete blocks, except that the number of appearances of each letter and the number of appearances of pairs need not be 4 and 1. A pair of letters does not need to be adjacent in the listing (as H, K in Block V) but only in the same block. The following is a very simple example in which each letter appears three times and each pair twice:

Block	Treatments
I	A, B, C
II	A, B, D
III	A, C, D
IV	B, C, D

For use, blocks should be taken in random order and treatments allotted at random to letters.

Many variants on these designs exist, mostly relaxations of the requirements of symmetry in order to permit greater adaptability to practical needs. Fully balanced designs exist for relatively few combinations of number of treatments, block size and replication (i.e. number of repetitions of each treatment). Alternatives in which the pairs are not equally represented or in which the blocks are not all of the same size can fill some of the gaps while still retaining enough symmetry to ensure that differences between treatment effects are estimated with nearly the same precision. Such designs are complicated in structure, but are widely used in many contexts, for example in field trials for comparing new varieties of an agricultural crop.

8.9 Factorial design

Another aspect of experimental design is concerned with the logical structure of the treatments. Suppose an investigator to be interested in the growth of a species of fish under controlled laboratory conditions. He has two strains of fish (S_1, S_2); he is interested in two different temperatures (T_1, T_2); he wishes to test two different concentrations of salt in the water (C_1, C_2). He could conduct three separate experiments, one comparing strains of fish, one comparing temperatures, and one comparing concentrations. For the experiment on strains, some combination of temperature and salt must be chosen; this may later turn out not to be the interesting combination, and a difference between S_1 and S_2 estimated under the conditions $T_2 C_2$ cannot be assumed applicable to $T_1 C_1$ or to $T_2 C_1$. Similar objections can be raised to each of the other two experiments.

A preferable alternative is to begin by recognizing all the $2 \times 2 \times 2$

treatment combinations:

$$
\begin{array}{ccc}
S_1 & T_1 & C_1 \\
S_2 & T_1 & C_1 \\
S_1 & T_2 & C_1 \\
S_2 & T_2 & C_1 \\
S_1 & T_1 & C_2 \\
S_2 & T_1 & C_2 \\
S_1 & T_2 & C_2 \\
S_2 & T_2 & C_2
\end{array}
$$

A single experiment can then compare all three *factors* simultaneously, using any design appropriate to 8 treatments and any constraints applicable to the circumstances – perhaps 5 randomized blocks of 8, or an 8×8 Latin square, or a balanced incomplete block design for 8 treatments in blocks of 4 (which requires 14 blocks and 7 'replicates' of each treatment). Such an experiment not only enables us to estimate average differences between strains, between temperatures, and between concentrations; it also allows study of whether the effect of concentration is affected by strain or by temperature and so on. These last comparisons are known as *interactions* of factors.

We here have a $2 \times 2 \times 2$ (or 2^3) factorial scheme of treatments. Had we had the same two strains but 3 temperatures and 3 concentrations, we should have had a $2 \times 3 \times 3$ (or 2×3^2) factorial scheme, 18 combinations in all. The possibilities are very numerous.

8.10* Confounding

One difficulty with factorial schemes is that the total number of treatment combinations can be very large – 4 factors each with only 3 levels produce 3^4 or 81 combinations. The suitable blocks commonly contain far fewer units. The device of *confounding* helps here, by ensuring that differences between blocks correspond to relatively uninteresting comparisons of treatments. Suppose that the laboratory in which the fish experiment in Section 8.9 was to be conducted had only four fish tanks with temperature control. Several distinct 'runs' would have to be conducted in successive periods, in order to include and to replicate the 8 treatment combinations. However, comparisons between results from different periods could be distorted because of unavoidable changes (e.g. source of food, initial size or origin of fish). The experiment can be organized into blocks of 4 in such a way that each block forms one run of 4 tanks, say for a 3-month period. Suitable blocks would be:

Block   I $S_1 T_1 C_1$, $S_1 T_2 C_2$, $S_2 T_1 C_2$, $S_2 T_2 C_1$
Block II $S_2 T_2 C_2$, $S_2 T_1 C_1$, $S_1 T_2 C_1$, $S_1 T_1 C_2$
Block III repeat I in a new random order
Block IV repeat II in a new random order
Block   V and so on (for any even number of blocks in all)

Write a, b, c, d, e, f, g, h as the mean values (e.g. increases in weight) for the treatment combinations in the order shown in Section 8.9, the mean being taken over all replicates. If there are 10 blocks in all, each combination will be repeated five times and f, for example, will be the mean for the 5 repetitions of $S_2 T_1 C_2$. Now consider

$$(-a + b - c + d - e + f - g + h)/4.$$

This average difference between all S_2 and all S_1 combinations involves 2 items from each block negatively and 2 positively and so is balanced over blocks; anything that causes one block to be particularly good or particularly bad for fish growth (e.g. a temporary change in food or in oxygenation) on average does not affect this quantity. Consider also

$$(-a - b + c + d - e - f + g + h)/4,$$
$$(-a - b - c - d + e + f + g + h)/4.$$

These are respectively the average difference between T_2 and T_1 and the average difference between C_2 and C_1, and they are similarly balanced over blocks.

The effect of temperature on strain 1 can be written

$$(-a + c - e + g)/2$$

and that on strain 2 is

$$(-b + d - f + h)/2.$$

Half the difference between these is a measure of whether the temperature change has a greater effect on S_2 than on S_1. After simplification it becomes:

$$(a - b - c + d + e - f - g + h)/4.$$

Had we looked instead at the difference between strains at temperature T_1

$$(-a + b - e + f)/2$$

and at T_2

$$(-c + d - g + h)/2,$$

and then taken half the difference of these, we should have obtained exactly the same quantity. This measures '*ST*', the interaction between strain and temperature. Again it is balanced over blocks, since a, d, f, g have contributions from Blocks I, III, V, . . . and two are taken positively, two negatively. Similar arguments lead to measures of interaction between strain and concentration (*SC*):

$$(a - b + c - d - e + f - g + h)/4,$$

and between temperature and concentration (*TC*):

$$(a + b - c - d - e - f + g + h)/4,$$

which have the same property of balance.

Finally we turn to an interaction of all three factors. A measure of *ST* interaction for C_1 alone is

$$(a - b - c + d)/2$$

and for C_2 alone is

$$(e - f - g + h)/2.$$

Half the difference between these simplifies to

$$(-a + b + c - d + e - f - g + h)/4.$$

You may like to verify that two other ways of starting (e.g. interaction *TC* for S_1 and S_2 separately) lead to the same thing. Now, however, the negative items (a, d, f, g) all come from Blocks I, III, V, . . . and the positives (b, c, e, h) all from Blocks II, IV, VI, ... Consequently this 3-factor interaction is also a measure of overall differences between blocks, something that may be inflated by external causes unconnected with the experimental treatments. We say that the 3-factor interaction *STC* is *confounded with block differences*. In practice, *STC* is almost always less interesting than the other effects and interactions, and so we may be content to sacrifice it in this way.

This must seem very complicated at first reading, but in fact it has a symmetric pattern and with experience is seen to be quite simple!

Look at the scheme of signs:

	a	b	c	d	e	f	g	h
S	−	+	−	+	−	+	−	+
T	−	−	+	+	−	−	+	+
ST	+	−	−	+	+	−	−	+
C	−	−	−	−	+	+	+	+
SC	+	−	+	−	−	+	−	+
TC	+	+	−	−	−	−	+	+
STC	−	+	+	−	+	−	−	+

Generalization to 4, 5, . . . factors is easy. There are important logical analogues in genetics. For the statistician, more interesting possibilities lie in further generalizations to factors with 3 or more levels, and these have been very thoroughly exploited for complex experiments. A related idea is that of *fractional replication*. An experiment on 7 factors at 2 levels each would involve 2^7, or 128, separate test units for even a single replicate of all treatment combinations. If the experimenter has reason to believe that the more complex interactions will be small and unimportant (and this is often so), he may be able to rest content with trying only a carefully chosen 64 or even 32 of the possibilities in a $\frac{1}{2}$ or $\frac{1}{4}$ replicate experiment. The price he pays is some uncertainty in inference: an effect he attributes to one factor might in reality be due to a complicated interaction of others.

Obviously confounding and fractional replication are devices needing great care. Used wisely, they permit limited experimental resources to give optimal information on many interacting factors; used without understanding, they can confuse the whole process of inference from experiments.

EXERCISES

(Regard Exercises 8.1–8.8 as a series of unusual puzzles. Do not try to find mathematical rules for solving them; the theory is complicated, and far more difficult than simply making a systematic search for a solution. The problems are deliberately presented without any biological context because of their generality; you should see how each can be related to experiments of the kinds mentioned in Sections 8.1, 8.4, 8.6 and 8.8.)

8.1 List all the ways in which the letters A, B, C can be arranged in a 3 × 3 Latin square.

8.2 Section 8.6 displays a 4 × 4 Graeco-Latin square. Note that the Roman letters alone constitute a Latin square, as do the Greek letters alone. Find a third Latin square, using the symbols w, x, y, z that, when superposed on the square in Section 8.6, has the properties (simultaneously): (i) large and small Roman letters form a Graeco-Latin, (ii) small Roman and Greek form a Graeco-Latin.

8.3 Consider the 5 × 5 Latin square

$$
\begin{array}{ccccc}
A & C & E & D & B \\
D & A & C & B & E \\
E & B & D & C & A \\
B & D & A & E & C \\
C & E & B & A & D
\end{array}
$$

Insert α, β, γ, δ, ε to convert this into a Graeco-Latin square.

8.4 Investigate the possibility of repeating Exercise 8.3 with the initial square

$$
\begin{array}{ccccc}
A & C & E & D & B \\
D & E & B & C & A \\
E & A & C & B & D \\
B & D & A & E & C \\
C & B & D & A & E
\end{array}
$$

(this question is more difficult).

8.5 From the letters A, B, C, D, E, F, G form 7 blocks of 4 so that
   (i) each of the different letters is used 4 times altogether, and
   (ii) every two *different* letters can be found in exactly 2 blocks.

   Thus you might start with AEFG; BDEG; etc. So far A has been used once, E twice; A and E have occurred once in the same block, E and G twice (i.e. in both blocks) and A and D have not yet occurred together. Alternatively, start with an arrangement in 7 blocks of 3, with each letter occurring 3 times and each pair in exactly one block. The solution needed consists of the complement of each block, the sets of 4 omitted letters.

8.6 Arrange your solution to Exercise 8.5 in a 7 × 4 formation, 7 columns of 4 entries, such that the entries in the columns constitute the 7 blocks of Exercise 8.5 and each row includes every letter once. If you were to begin in the way suggested above, you could try to complete:

D	G	E	A	F	C	B
+	+	G	+	+	+	D
+	+	F	+	+	+	G
+	+	A	+	+	+	E

8.7 (from *New Scientist*, 31 March 1977)

Burpwater's Best is not the greatest of beers and is to be had only in the five pubs owned by the brewery. The customers are so rude about it that the landlords keep putting in for transfers. Until four years ago these requests were always refused but there was then a change of policy, resulting in annual reshuffles. Now, after four such upheavals, each landlord has had a disgruntled go at running four of the pubs and is at present ensconced in the fifth.

Patrick's first move was from the Duck to the Anchor and his next to the Cormorant. This second shuffle took Quentin to the Eagle and Roger to the pub previously run by Tony. At the third move Tony handed the Bull over to Roger, who took over from Simon at the following move. Where is each gloomy publican to be found now?

8.8 With the aid of Exercise 8.2, determine how 20 blocks of 4 letters can be formed, using only the 16 letters A, B, C, . . . , N, O, P, such that

(i) each of the 16 letters is used 5 times altogether,

and (ii) every two different letters can be found in exactly one of the 16 blocks.

8.9 The first t letters of the alphabet are arranged in sets of 3 in such a way that:

(i) each letter appears r times in all;

(ii) the 'pairs of letters in the same set' (if A, J, L is a set, the three pairs are AJ, AL, JL) totalled over all sets include every possible pair p times each.

Construct an example for $t = 4$. Prove that, for any t, $rt/3$ is an integer; what does this integer represent? Prove that $p = 2r/(t - 1)$.

8.10 Plants of a certain species show early signs of serious attack by a fungus. Fourteen plants are chosen at random for testing seven different fungicides (denoted by A, B, C, D, E, F, G), each of which can be applied to a single leaf. On the first plant, the three lowest leaves are designated to receive fungicides C, D, F in order from the foot of the stem; on the second plant, the corresponding three leaves will receive fungicides D, E, G. Note that the second 3 letters are an alphabetic shift of 1 letter from the first 3; similarly, the third plant has fungicides E, F, A (because only 7 letters are required, the letter G shifts to A). This process continues until treatments are specified for the three leaves on each of the 14 plants. After a prescribed time, a record is made of proportionate fungal damage to each of the 42 leaves. Write out the full set of treatment specifications for the first, second, and third leaf on every plant. Comment briefly on the symmetries in the design and how they help to balance differences of leaf position and differences between plants. State the advantages and disadvantages of this design over the alternative of treating 2 plants entirely with A, 2 with B, and so on.

9 Comparisons between means

9.1 The need

We have not yet dealt adequately with the Gopain data. Chapter 7 discussed standard errors for a single mean and probabilistic inference based on this. Section 8.2 indicated how the methods of Chapter 7 can be used in a paired comparison experiment, but this is no help for Table 1.1 which had no planned pairing and unequal numbers in series D, E. We must consider what can be said about differences between means, their appropriate standard errors and subsequent probability statements, when the means are based on unequal numbers of observations. We need also to ask how this applies to the more complicated experimental designs of Chapter 8, where several treatments are under test simultaneously and various constraints on the organization and randomization of the experiment are deliberately introduced.

9.2 Examples of treatments

Many kinds of investigation can call for a comparison of results for two 'treatments' that is logically similar to that described in Section 1.2. For example:

(i) The Gopain problem of Chapter 1 (human or mouse version);
(ii) Blood pressures of dogs, some having received a certain drug and some (often described as 'controls') having had no drug;
(iii) Yields of apple trees under two different systems of pruning;
(iv) Frequencies of a specified deformity in *Drosophila* from parent flies exposed to radiation and from untreated stock;
(v) Weights of seed per plant from individuals of a species collected in two different environments.

The word 'treatment' is a convenient and well-established general term even where in strict logic it may seem inappropriate. It is used not only for a system of pruning, as in (iii) where two systems are to be compared, but also for a null state – absence of drug in (ii), absence of radiation in (iv). In (v), nothing is truly 'treated', but use is made of naturally occurring contrasted environments, say a valley floor and a plateau at 250 metres above the valley; a comparison between breeds of animal, between male and female speeds of reaction, or between smokers and non-smokers is similar because the categories have occurred and are not determined by act of the investigator. Often more than two treatments are included in one experiment (cf. Chapter 8), for economic and other reasons. In most circumstances, only a very unimaginative investigator could fail to be interested in more than two treatments or categories. If A, B, C, D are all of interest, separate studies of different pairs of treatments would usually require far more materials, time and labour than a single carefully planned study of all at once, although almost inevitably the latter will be larger and more expensive than any one comparison of a pair. Typical needs are to compare:

(vi) Effects on mice of doses 0.0, 1.0, 2.0, 3.0 units of Gopain;
(vii) Growth rates of plants in 5 different types of pot;
(viii) Milk productions of cattle receiving a standard diet or a diet with one of 4 different protein supplements;
(ix) Reading skills of primary school children under three different methods of instruction;
(x) Growth of bacterial cultures exposed to three different doses of two different antibiotics (i.e., 6 combinations of treatment).

Although very commonly the number of observations will be the same for each treatment (especially if one of the more sophisticated experimental designs of Chapter 8 is used), this is not always so. Just as Table 1.1 had 7 subjects on one treatment, 5 on another, so research on (vii) above might have 12, 4, 9, 15, 6 plants in the five types of pot (but see Section 9.8).

9.3 Experiments and non-experiments

In a genuine experiment, the investigator decides which units (plants, animals, cultures, machines, etc.) shall be assigned to each treatment. By adopting a random allocation, he ensures that no distortion of estimates of treatment effects can arise from unconscious (or conscious) biases – giving the best animals to a favourite treatment, etc. For a simple experiment, randomization requires some form of fair lottery (spinning coins, drawing cards, using published tables of random digits, etc.). Some of the designs in Chapter 8 call for greater care, and at your first encounter you will need advice from a statistician.

In a non-experimental situation, randomizing is impossible. In (v) of Section 9.2, plants from a common source may be placed in the two environments after random allocation; a more likely approach is that an ecologist visits the valley and the plateau and collects seeds from the natural flora. In Section 1.2, there could be no question of subjecting randomly chosen subjects to unnecessary surgery in order to give them specified Gopain experience! Although statistical analysis may still show a difference between treatments, the cause of a difference cannot be uncritically attributed to the stated treatments. If the plateau plants produce less seed, this may be because of their harsher environment or because they are of different origin and genetically less productive. Repeated exposure to Gopain may increase the liability to jaundice, but alternatively observers may be more alert to noticing jaundice occurring soon after a multiple exposure; just possibly, persons with an inherent liability to jaundice may be more liable to need the forms of surgery for which Gopain is given. The controversy on smoking as a cause of lung cancer and other ills has dragged on for years largely because of this kind of difficulty.

When interpreting apparent effects of treatments in a non-experiment, remember that statistics alone cannot discriminate between alternative explanations. If data are abundant a deeper analysis may help, but great caution is essential.

9.4 Symbols

Full analysis of the problem of two means is not inherently more difficult than that in Section 7.3, but for ease of presentation it requires an extended symbolism which will also be applicable to a greater number of treatments. Suppose that the two groups contain n_1, n_2 observations; for the Gopain data, we had $n_1 = 7, n_2 = 5$. Write y_{1j} $(j = 1, 2, \ldots, n_1)$ for the observations in the first group, and similarly y_{2j} for the second. You will frequently meet this kind of notation (and generalizations of it) for mathematical, scientific and computational purposes. In computer use $Y(I, J)$, analogous to our present y_{ij}, is commonly used to represent item J of information in a category I. For our purpose, we write the population mean of the variate for the group of observations identified by i as

$$E(y_{ij}|i \text{ fixed}) = \mu_i, \qquad [9.\text{I}]$$

with $i = 1, 2$. The possibility of extending to $i = 1, 2, 3, \ldots$ should be obvious. Also write the sample means

$$\bar{y}_1 = \left[\sum_{j=1}^{n_1} y_{1j} \right] \bigg/ n_1, \bar{y}_2 = \left[\sum_{j=1}^{n_2} y_{2j} \right] \bigg/ n_2. \qquad [9.\text{II}]$$

For example, in (ii) of Section 9.2, μ_1 is the mean blood pressure for a population of dogs receiving the drug, μ_2 is the mean that the same population would show in the absence of the drug, and $\bar{y}_1$, $\bar{y}_2$ are means of n_1, n_2 dogs included in an experiment. Unless the treatments have a very large difference in effect, we are usually safe to write

$$Var(y_{ij}) = \sigma^2, \qquad [9.\text{III}]$$

a constant for all i, j. From Section 6.2, we know that

$$E(\bar{y}_1) = \mu_1, \quad E(\bar{y}_2) = \mu_2, \qquad [9.\text{IV}]$$
$$Var(\bar{y}_1) = \sigma^2/n_1, \quad Var(\bar{y}_2) = \sigma^2/n_2. \qquad [9.\text{V}]$$

9.5 Difference of two means

Suppose we define

$$\lambda = \mu_1 - \mu_2;$$

then λ is a new parameter (any function of parameters alone can always be regarded as itself being a parameter). It measures the amount by which the expected mean of an observation is changed when treatment 1 replaces treatment 2. By Equation [9.IV], and of course appeal to Equation [5.XIV], we see that

$$E(\bar{y}_1 - \bar{y}_2) = \lambda. \qquad [9.\text{VI}]$$

Thus $(\bar{y}_1 - \bar{y}_2)$, the obvious statistic to use, is an unbiased estimator of the parameter that interests us. Exercise 7.3 illustrated, somewhat artificially, a general formula that now becomes vitally important:

$$Var(\bar{y}_1 - \bar{y}_2) = Var(\bar{y}_1) + Var(\bar{y}_2). \qquad [9.\text{VII}]$$

This can be proved by extension of the algebra required for proving

Equation [6.I] (cf. Section 6.4). Here it becomes

$$Var(\bar{y}_1 - \bar{y}_2) = \sigma^2\left(\frac{1}{n_1} + \frac{1}{n_2}\right) \qquad [9.VIII]$$

Moreover, if we have a value for s^2, an estimate of σ^2, we can estimate $Var(\bar{y}_1 - \bar{y}_2)$ by

$$s^2\left[\frac{1}{n_1} + \frac{1}{n_2}\right]. \qquad [9.IX]$$

I need not repeat the discussion of Normal and t-distributions from Chapters 6 and 7. Under similar conditions, inference on λ can be based on the t-distribution. The exact form of this will be apparent from the analysis of Table 1.1 that follows.

9.6 Gopain again

Preliminary calculations for a final analysis of the Gopain problem, already completed in Exercise 6.3, can be summarized in our new symbols as (for D):

$$n_1 = 7,$$
$$\bar{y}_1 = 84/7 = 12.0,$$
$$\sum y_{1j}^2 = 1218,$$
$$\sum (y_{1j}^2 - \bar{y}_1)^2 = 1218 - 84^2/7 = 210.0.$$

Similarly for E:

$$n_2 = 5,$$
$$\bar{y}_2 = 30/5 = 6.0,$$
$$\sum (y_{2j} - \bar{y}_2)^2 = 50.0.$$

You should check this arithmetic. Two sums of squares of deviations now give information on σ^2, 210.0 with 6 d.f. and 50.0 with 4 d.f. To obtain a single estimate, we should give greater weight to the information with the larger number of d.f. If we had estimates based on 150 d.f. and 2 d.f. respectively, to form a simple average of the two s^2 values would be ridiculous, as it would take no account of the far greater trustworthiness of an estimate from 151 observations than of one from only 3 observations. Fortunately the correct rule for combination is very simple:

$$s^2 = \frac{\text{Total of } \sum(y - \bar{y})^2}{\text{Total of d.f.}}, \qquad [9.X]$$

and s^2 now has the number of d.f. in its denominator. Here

$$s^2 = \frac{210.0 + 50.0}{6 + 4}$$

$$= \frac{260.0}{10}$$

$$= 26.0, \quad \text{with 10 d.f.}$$

When t was defined in Equation [6.II] and extended so as to use an estimated variance in Equation [7.I], only the special forms appropriate to a single sample of observations were displayed. In fact the theory simply requires that

$$t = \frac{\text{Deviation from expectation}}{\text{SE}}, \qquad [9.XI]$$

subject only to the conditions that the deviation referred to is that of some combination of means of Normally distributed observations and its SE is calculated according to the appropriate rules from σ^2 or s^2. If we knew the Gopain σ^2, we should work in terms of a generalization of Equation [6.II]

$$t = \frac{\bar{y}_1 - \bar{y}_2 - \lambda}{\sqrt{[\sigma^2(1/n_1 + 1/n_2)]}}, \qquad [9.XII]$$

and refer to values of t for $N(0, 1)$ in Table 6.1. Here we replace the unknown σ^2 by s^2 and use the t-distribution with 10 d.f. from Table 7.1 with the corresponding generalization of Equation [7.I]:

$$t_{10} = \frac{12.0 - 6.0 - \lambda}{\sqrt{[26.0(1/7 + 1/5)]}}$$

$$= \frac{6.0 - \lambda}{\sqrt{8.91}}.$$

The value from Table 7.1 is 2.23, and therefore

$$Pr\left(-2.23 \leqslant \frac{6.0 - \lambda}{2.98} \leqslant 2.23\right) = 0.95,$$

from which we obtain lower and upper limits to λ at probability 0.95:

$$\lambda_L = 6.0 - 2.23 \times 2.98 = -0.6,$$
$$\lambda_U = 6.0 + 2.23 \times 2.98 = 12.6.$$

In asserting that, with probability 0.95, the difference between the true means for D and E lies between -0.6 days and 12.6 days, we clearly include 0.0 days as a possibility. The evidence of the data is not sufficiently strong to exclude a belief that on average the time to jaundice is independent of whether the patient has had one or two exposures to Gopain. As in Section 7.5, we may write in terms of the standard error:

Estimated difference of means $= 6.0 \pm 2.98$.

The above may seem a very condensed account of the method, but in fact the calculations are a repetition of those in Sections 7.2 and 7.3 except for the introduction of Equations [9.X] and [9.XII].

9.7 Statistical significance

One of the commonest forms of statistical jargon involves the words 'statistically significant'. I have purposely avoided it except in Section 4.2, because I believe the ideas of fiducial or confidence limits to be more valuable and more easily understood, but I must now turn to it: you should re-read Sections 4.1 and 4.2. Suppose I state a null hypothesis (NH): 'Time to occurrence of an attack of jaundice is unaffected by whether a patient has had one or two exposures to Gopain.' This is a statement about the population, in fact a statement that $\mu_1 = \mu_2$ or $\lambda = 0$. A test of statistical significance examines the plausibility of this hypothesis in the light of the evidence, and rejects the hypothesis if belief in it would demand that a very improbable event has occurred. Insertion of $\lambda = 0$ into the numerical expression for t in Section 9.6 gives

$$t_{10} = \frac{6.0}{2.98} = 2.01.$$

This does not exceed the value for probability 0.95 and 10 d.f. in Table 7.1, so showing that the probability of a deviation from λ as great as or greater than 6.0 exceeds $(1.00 - 0.95)$; the exact probability could be found from more detailed tables if required. The deviation is said to be not *statistically significant*. Truth of the hypothesis does not require belief that a rare event (probability less than 0.05) has occurred, and the hypothesis is not rejected. You must on no account fall into the common trap of concluding that the test has proved the NH true; in reality we merely conclude that one particular hypothesis does not predict data very different from those observed. We could formulate many other NH about the difference between the times to jaundice under the two conditions, for example $\lambda = -0.2$ or $\lambda = 0.43$. With $\lambda = 0.43$

$$t_{10} = \frac{6.0 - 0.43}{2.98} = 1.87,$$

and again the deviation is found not statistically significant. The same set of data cannot prove the truth of several hypotheses: all that happens is that none of them is rejected as untrue.

Note the close relation between significance tests and the previous calculations of limits. The interval -0.6 to 12.6 includes all values for λ that would not be rejected as null hypotheses by a significance test at probability 0.05. The fact that the interval includes 0.0 is logically equivalent to the statement that the data do not deviate from a NH that $\lambda = 0$ to an extent that is judged statistically significant.

For a moment suppose that all the D data had been 2 days longer than in Table 1.1, with E unaltered. Then we should have:

Estimated difference of means $= 8.0 \pm 2.98$.

Calculations as before give limits

$$8.0 - 2.23 \times 2.98 = 1.6,$$
$$8.0 + 2.23 \times 2.98 = 14.6.$$

When we assert that, with probability 0.95, λ lies between 1.4 and 14.6, we clearly exclude 0.0; we reject any statement that D and E do not differ. If we again state $\lambda = 0$ as our NH, then

$$t = \frac{8.0}{2.98} = 2.7,$$

which exceeds the value 2.23 tabulated for a probability of 0.95. Hence there is a probability less than 0.05 that a difference as great as or greater than 8.0 is observed if the null hypothesis is true. We express this by saying that, at probability 0.05, $(\bar{y}_1 - \bar{y}_2)$ shows a *statistically significant* deviation from the value zero implied by the null hypothesis.

Let me remind you that, as a convention, I have throughout calculated limits at probability 0.95 and correspondingly tested significance at probability 0.05. I could have used 0.99 and 0.01, or for that matter 0.877 and 0.123, the only change being in my level of assurance in asserting conclusions. The choice is for the user to make in relation to the degree of assurance he wishes to have, but in the absence of clear reasons to the contrary adherence to a conventional practice seems desirable.

9.8 Allocation of experimental units

An experimental scientist often needs to decide how many animals or other units he will allocate to each treatment, within the constraint that his total is fixed by consideration of costs, availability, space, etc. Look back at $Var(\bar{y}_1 - \bar{y}_2)$ in Equation [9.VIII]. Suppose we are prepared to make 12 observations in all, but (as in the mouse experiment of Section 1.4) we have freedom to decide how many shall be in each group. Thus we must have

$$n_1 + n_2 = 12$$

and of course

$$n_1 \geqslant 1, \quad n_2 \geqslant 1.$$

The factor σ^2 is unaltered by the choice of n_1, but $Var(\bar{y}_1 - \bar{y}_2)$ clearly depends upon whether the second factor is

$$\left(\frac{1}{11} + \frac{1}{1}\right) \quad or \quad \left(\frac{1}{10} + \frac{1}{2}\right) \quad or \quad \left(\frac{1}{7} + \frac{1}{5}\right) \quad or \quad \left(\frac{1}{2} + \frac{1}{10}\right).$$

It is easily proved, as should seem intuitively reasonable, that we have a minimum when $n_1 = n_2 = 6$. The result is general. Under the condition that the total number of observations is fixed, the variance of the difference between two means is least when the groups are equal in number. A small departure from equality matters very little:

$$\frac{1}{6} + \frac{1}{6} = 0.333$$

but

$$\frac{1}{7} + \frac{1}{5} = 0.343.$$

Consequently, if the total is odd, say 23, the slight inequality of a division into 12, 11 or 11, 12 does not represent much loss relative to the ideal.

9.9* Estimation of variance for several treatments

Some of the results for two treatments generalize easily. In particular, Equation [9.X] applies to any number of groups that share a common σ^2, provided that the design has no randomized block or other structure. Thus the experiment mentioned at the end of Section 9.2 would give five sums of squares of deviations with 11, 3, 8, 14, 5 d.f., which could be combined by Equation [9.X] to yield s^2 with 41 d.f.; this could be used in examining differences between treatment means. The rule of Section 9.8 also generalizes in an obvious manner. If all comparisons are equally interesting to the investigator, equal allocation of units to treatments is optimal. The experiment just mentioned had 46 plants in all: these would have been better allocated as 10 to one of the five treatments and 9 to each of the others. With three or more treatments, however, other objectives (such as special emphasis on particular comparisons) may call for different optimal allocations.

As indicated in Section 8.3, a technique known as analysis of variance is widely used for the analysis of data on continuous variates. For all the designs of Chapter 8 and many others, it is the standard procedure for extracting an estimate of variance per observation, a value of s^2 that estimates σ^2 from the complex data. It takes the sum of squares of deviations from the mean for all the data, isolates parts of this as corresponding to assignable sources (mainly effects of treatments) or to irrelevant variations (between blocks in Section 8.3, between rows and between columns in Section 8.4, and so on), and leaves a residual with a known number of d.f. from which a mean square, s^2 is formed. It provides an alternative route to Equation [9.X] in the simple experiments for which that is appropriate, it includes the basic calculations of Section 9.6 as a special case, and it is one of the most powerful tools of statistical analysis for wide application to experimental and non-experimental records. I shall illustrate the analysis of variance for a randomized block experiment, though I cannot give much explanation here.

Table 9.1 contains data from a trial of three different baits for catching fruit flies. Three baited traps were exposed at each of 7 sites, the types of bait being allocated at random to the 3 positions at each site. The figures recorded are the numbers of flies caught in a fixed time interval. The data are taken from a larger experiment [*Biometrics* **8** (1952) p. 383]. I have excluded a fourth bait, which gave much smaller and less variable catches, because no formal analysis was necessary to demonstrate that it was less effective, and I have retained only 7 of 12 sites in order to reduce the arithmetic for any reader who cares to repeat the calculations. Insect counts are discrete and therefore cannot conform to a Normal distribution, but when the

Table 9.1 Results of an experiment on baits for catching fruit flies
(numbers of flies caught)

Site	Bait B	C	D	Total
I	75	41	47	163
II	52	30	29	111
III	58	38	25	121
IV	19	20	10	49
V	34	28	13	75
VI	33	26	17	76
VII	25	15	12	52
Total	296	198	153	647

numbers are fairly large this can often be safely ignored. Some statistical texts would advise an analysis based on the square roots or the logarithms of the counts; I am concerned only with a simple illustration, but I suggest that anyone encountering an analogous problem in this work would be wise to consult a statistician about this question of transforming data before analysis.

Table 9.1 is bordered by totals of counts at each site and counts for each bait. The first step in the analysis of variance is to form:

Adjustment for mean = (grand total)^2/number of observations
$$= 647^2/21 = 19933.76.$$

Now find the total sum of squares of observations, as in Equation [5.IX]

$$75^2 + 41^2 + 47^2 + 52^2 + \ldots + 15^2 + 12^2 - 647^2/21 = 5477.24,$$

with 20 d.f. Variation between sites is irrelevant to the comparison of baits since the experimental design has ensured a balance over sites. Therefore a sum of squares between sites, scaled to allow for the fact that each site total comprises 3 counts, must be deducted from the figure just calculated:

$$(163^2 + 111^2 + \ldots + 52^2)/3 - 647^2/21 = 3411.91,$$

with $(7-1)$ d.f. The sum of squares between baits is similarly calculated from bait totals, the number of counts per bait, 7, now appearing as a divisor:

$$(296^2 + 198^2 + 153^2)/7 - 647^2/21 = 1527.52,$$

with $(3-1)$ d.f. The error sum of squares and its number of degrees of freedom (12) are now obtained by subtractions that make the first three items in Table 9.2 add to the fourth.

Table 9.2 Analysis of variance for Table 9.1

| Adjustment for mean | | 19 933.76 | |
Source of variation	*d.f.*	*Sum of squares*	*Mean square*
Blocks	6	3 411.91	
Treatments	2	1 527.52	
Error	12	537.81	44.82
Total	20	5 477.24	

Division of the error sum of squares by its d.f. yields a mean square which is a generalization of Equation [9.X] and which is the appropriate s^2 to be used in comparisons between baits. With it we can proceed exactly as in Section 9.7. For example, the means for B, C are

$$\bar{y}_B = 42.3, \quad \bar{y}_C = 28.3,$$

and by Equation [9.IX] we estimate

$$Var(\bar{y}_A - \bar{y}_B) = 44.82 \times \left(\frac{1}{7} + \frac{1}{7}\right)$$
$$= (3.58)^2 \quad \text{with} \quad 12 \text{ d.f.}$$

The *t*-statistic for the null hypothesis that the true means differ by λ has 12 d.f., the number of d.f. for s^2. Hence

$$t = \frac{14.0 - \lambda}{3.58}.$$

The 0.95 probability value of t from an enlarged Table 7.1 is 2.18, from which limits for λ are calculated as 6.2, 21.8, convincing evidence that $\lambda = 0$ should be rejected and that bait B is significantly more successful than C. For bait D,

$$\bar{y}_D = 21.9.$$

In comparing C and D, exactly the same variance applies,

$$t_{12} = \frac{6.4 - \lambda}{3.58};$$

the limits are calculated as -1.4, 14.2. Hence the NH that C and D are equally effective baits is not contradicted, despite the fact that C had the higher catch at 6 of the 7 sites. Of course one should not conclude that D is as good as C, only that the evidence does not suffice to dismiss this hypothesis.

This valuable method of analysis is immensely adaptable. Had the fly-bait experiment been designed merely as 7 traps of each treatment, randomly allocated among 21 positions with no classification by site, the calculations would have been modified by not calculating a sum of squares for blocks and so having 18 d.f. for error. The analysis would then become equivalent to that outlined in the first paragraph of this section. The error mean square would almost centainly have been larger on account of omission of any balancing over sites. For a Latin square design (not relevant to this example), 'Blocks' would be replaced by independent sums of squares for 'Rows' and 'Columns', so taking account of the balance imposed simultaneously in two directions. To each of the other designs in Chapter 8 there corresponds an analysis of variance, but calculation of such analyses should not be attempted by the novice without advice from a statistician.

When more than two treatments are being studied, often they (or some of them) are defined by an ascending scale of another variate – in the examples of Section 9.2, dose of Gopain in (vi), daily intake of protein in (viii), concentration of antibiotic in (x). The relation between y and this other variate, x, almost invariably needs examination. A diagram to show the mean of y at each value of x and to draw this should be standard practice; I return to the problem in Section 10.2.

EXERCISES

9.1 Eleven seedlings in individual pots are divided at random into two groups of 5 and 6. The first group is grown in normal light, the second in restricted light. After 4 months, the heights (in cm) of the plants are:

Normal	Restricted
46	39
39	28
38	31
41	37
36	41
	34

Examine the evidence against the null hypothesis: 'Restricting the light does not affect the height of this species of plant.' Obtain limits to the difference of population means at probability 0.95 (with 9 d.f., the 0.95 level of t is 2.26): use very approximate arithmetic for square roots.

9.2 Repeat the calculations for the heights

Normal: 38, 40, 38, 43, 41
Restricted: 34, 32, 34, 37, 35, 38.

9.3 Repeat the calculations for the heights

Normal: 59, 17, 29, 62, 33
Restricted: 18, 60, 27, 25, 42, 38.

9.4 A new experiment had 10 plants in normal light, 12 plants restricted. By chance, the results were like those in Exercise 9.1 with each height in the earlier experiment repeated twice. Without doing the arithmetic, discuss, approximately, the new conclusions.

9.5 From each of 5 litters of an animal species, two males were taken for an experiment. A randomly selected member of each pair received a diet lacking an important constituent, and its littermate received a standard 'control' diet. Each animal was weighed at the start and again after 6 weeks. The weight changes (kg) were:

Litter	Control	Deficient
I	+ 2.8	+ 1.4
II	+ 0.7	− 0.2
III	+ 1.2	+ 0.1
IV	+ 1.5	+ 0.0
V	+ 0.4	− 0.7

Estimate the mean effect of the dietary deficiency, as a change in weight gain, in kg per animal. Find a standard error for this estimate, and calculate limits within which the true effect lies with probability 0.95.

9.6 An entomologist is investigating whether an insect pest is as plentiful on a variety of a plant species with rough leaves as on another variety with smooth leaves. He grows five plants of each variety in adjacent positions and counts the number of insects on each. Unfortunately he mislays the records of one of the 'smooth' plants. For the remaining 9 plants, he obtains mean counts of 48.5 (smooth) and 37.2 (rough), and routine calculations lead to $t = 2.65$ with 7 d.f. This value of t is 'statistically significant at a probability of 0.05'. The entomologist then finds the missing record, a count of 110 for the fifth smooth plant. What is now the mean number of insects per smooth plant? When he repeats the calculations, the entomologist finds a value of t (now with 8 d.f.) smaller than before and not statistically significant. Comment on his surprise and suggest an explanation.

10 Additional topics

I shall end by brief remarks about a number of topics that are too important to the practice of statistics in biology to be neglected but that cannot be discussed at all fully in an introductory book.

10.1 Sampling

A biologist often needs to estimate some property of a population, not with a view to experimental comparisons but as part of a descriptive and quantitative study of the population or as a step towards a decision. For example:

   (i) How many caterpillars per cabbage are there in a certain field?
  (ii) What is the mean weight of 8-year old girls?
 (iii) How many deer live in a tract of forest?
 (iv) What proportion of trees in city gardens are over 15 m tall?
  (v) What is the mean length of hospital stay for patients admitted after traffic accidents?

The computational and logical requirements are commonly much as in previous chapters. For example, from weights of a sample of children one can calculate a mean, and from the sum of squares of deviations from that mean one can obtain an estimated SE and then limits for the population mean at any desired probability. However, the manner in which the sample was acquired is usually very important and attention to random selection can be vital. Choosing children from one school may bias results because that school serves a prosperous and well-nourished community; children markedly underweight may be more subject to illnesses that cause absence from school on the day chosen for weighing. Cabbages near the edge of the field can be picked for a sample most easily, but their closeness to external sources of infection may make them especially liable to attack by some pests and diseases.

Statisticians have developed many techniques for improving the precision of estimates from samples. Perhaps most important is *stratification*, the dividing of a heterogeneous population into strata that are likely to be more uniform; each stratum is then sampled separately, and the separate stratum estimates are eventually combined into the required population estimate. For example, by subdividing a city into localities, strata with predominantly small or new gardens and therefore few tall trees could be separated from those with large and old gardens. Patients in hospital after accidents could be divided into strata of those suffering only from shock and therefore not needing to stay long, those with minor injuries, and those with severe injuries or requiring major surgery. Another group of techniques takes advantage of the possibility that some types of measurement are made more easily and cheaply than others. Interest may lie in the number of seeds produced by a species of plant; if the numbers are large, harvesting and counting can be very laborious, whereas counts of seed capsules or flowers can be made much more easily. By determining both quantities for some plants and the number of capsules only for a far larger sample, the relation between seed and capsule number can be exploited to increase the precision achieved in relation to the effort expended. These and other devices relate to the design of sampling investigations. The statistical analysis in its simplest form is essentially that of Section 7.3, but more complex designs require more elaborate variance formulae.

Among sampling techniques of special interest to biologists is that of recapture sampling. It is used for estimating the number of individuals in a population of living organisms. A random sample of animals (or birds or fishes or insects) is caught, each member is given a distinguishing mark, and all are returned to the population. Suppose that 200 marked individuals are so returned, and that a subsequent new random sample of 500 is found to contain 25 bearing the mark; since only 1/8 of the marks have been recovered, the total population is estimated to contain 8×500 individuals. Clearly there are simplifying assumptions about absence of immigration, emigration, birth and death, and about the mixing of marked with non-marked. Many refinements have been developed, and this type of sampling, extensively used by ecologists, is a large topic in its own right.

10.2* Regression and correlation

The biologist is often concerned with the relation between two or more variates. Many new problems then call for consideration, with complexities far beyond the range of this book. One common situation has already been mentioned in Section 9.9. 'Doses' of one variate, for which the symbol x is commonly used, are chosen, and several values of y are measured at each x. The dose might be the amount of Gopain administered, the temperature at which a plant is grown, the daily ration of protein to a calf, or the dose of radiation given to *Drosophila* in a study of mutations. A natural and helpful first step is to plot values of y (perhaps plant heights) against x (temperature); the variate whose values are chosen by the investigator, the so-called *independent variate*, is by convention put on the horizontal scale.

Figures 10.1–10.4 illustrate some of the types of diagram that may result. Even for the one problem of relating plant growth to temperature, all of these and more could be encountered, the form perhaps varying from one species to another or being dependent on other factors such as fertilizer or water supply. I assume here that attention is being restricted to moderate temperatures, well between the extremes at which cold or heat would prevent all growth. Provided that the nature of the dependence of y on x can be specified, appropriate parameters can be estimated from the data. The usual approach is to think in terms of the expectation of y for a fixed x, that is to say the mean of the sub-population of y for which x has the

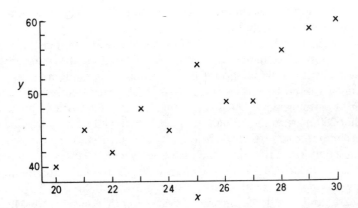

Figure 10.1. Set of eleven (x, y) points showing a roughly linear regression of y on x.

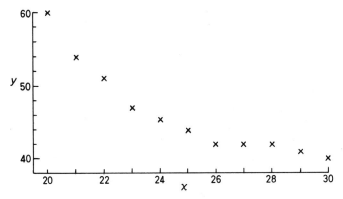

Figure 10.2. Set of eleven (x, y) points showing a curvilinear regression of y on x.

particular value. If these expectations were known and could be plotted against x, they would define a curve that is known as the *regression curve* of y on x.

The simplest form of regression is that in which the curve is a straight line. Instead of having

$$E(y) = \mu,$$

as in Section 5.5 we have

$$E(y) = \alpha + \beta x, \qquad [10.\text{I}]$$

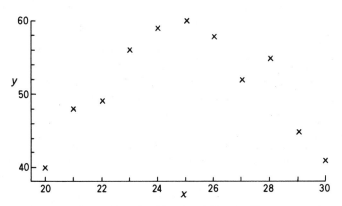

Figure 10.3 Set of eleven (x, y) points showing a curvilinear regression of y on x with a maximum.

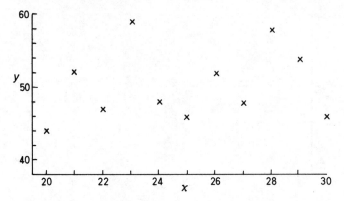

Figure 10.4. Set of eleven (x, y) points showing y independent of x.

the equation to a straight line. This states that at $x = 0$ the expectation of y is α and that the expectation increases by β for each unit increase in x. Often one can regard the SD and the variance of y about its expectation as constant, which makes possible simple computations for finding the best numerical values to use as estimates of α and β. The detail is beyond my present objectives, but the broad principle should be clear. Of course, a regression curve need not be as simple as a straight line. Figure 10.2 might be better fitted by a quadratic equation:

$$E(y) = \alpha + \beta x + \gamma x^2;$$

many other equations are suited to special circumstances. For example,

$$E(y) = \alpha + \beta \log x$$

is useful if the effect of a fixed proportionate increase in x (such as doubling x) is believed to be independent of x, by contrast with Equation [10.I] where a fixed absolute increase in x has the same effect whatever the x with which we start; the equation

$$E(y) = \alpha - \beta \times 10^{-\gamma x}$$

is useful if the expectation of y is expected to be rising steeply with x when x is small but to level off and approach a constant as x becomes large.

For the example of growth and temperature, there is no question about which is the independent and which the dependent variate: no one would propose to use a regression of temperature on growth.

With other types of data, such as those obtained when both x and y are measurements of size on individual organisms, two regressions may be of interest. For instance, in a human population one might have records of weight and systolic blood pressure. It is now potentially interesting to examine the expectation of y for fixed x and also the expectation of x for fixed y. The two regression curves are not identical (even when each is a straight line, the two lines are distinct), and they describe different features of the data. This distinction is vitally important; it is a cause of much confusion, but unfortunately it will not disappear in response to the intuitive comment 'Well I don't see why the two regressions are not the same'! Contrary to what is commonly believed, the choice of whether y or x is to be regarded as the dependent variate is not determined by which variate is to be estimated. Even though the purpose is to estimate the temperature corresponding to a specified value of the growth variate, the appropriate regression is that of growth on temperature. Suppose that the ages and heights of a large number of children are recorded, and that 10-year olds have a mean height of 133 cm. The question 'At what age is the mean height 133 cm?' certainly has the answer '10-years'; the question 'What is the mean age of children whose present height is 133 cm?' is totally different and only exceptionally will give the same answer. If a set of data are such that both regression curves are meaningful, the choice for a particular problem may be difficult; the important factor is the *error structure*, the formulae known or assumed to relate data to expectations.

The study of regression has many uses, among which are:

  (i) It aids the simple description of data;
 (ii) It enables values of y to be predicted for values of x other than those in the data (but *not* beyond the range of the data);
(iii) It makes possible the estimation of the value of x at which y will have a specified expectation;
 (iv) It sometimes allows the precision of experimental comparisons of y for different treatments to be increased by adjustment for inequalities in a second variate x, by the *analysis of covariance* (a generalization of the analysis of variance);
  (v) It sometimes allows the difference between sets of values of y to be expressed simply by a difference or ratio of values of x for which expectations of y are identical (biological assay and associated techniques);

(vi) When the regression is curvilinear, it may be used for estimating the value of x that maximizes (or minimizes) the expectation of y.

You must always beware of making inferences from a regression outside the range of values from which the parameters are estimated. The increase in plant height in 6 weeks from seed germination might show a very good linear regression on temperature between 15° C and 30° C. This could be used to predict the growth of a plant grown under the same conditions at 23.5° C, but prediction would be dangerous at 35° C and ridiculous at 130° C or − 20° C. The theory and practice of regression can be extended to several independent variates; for example, a regression equation might represent the dependence of the root-weight of a plant on several properties of the soil (pH, phosphate content, % clay, height above sea-level) simultaneously.

Related to regression, but measuring something quite different, is the *correlation coefficient*. If pairs of x, y are defined for a number of individuals (plants, insects, cells, cities), the correlation coefficient is defined as

$$r = \frac{\Sigma (x - \bar{x})(y - \bar{y})}{\sqrt{[\Sigma (x - \bar{x})^2 \, \Sigma (y - \bar{y})^2]}}. \qquad [10.II]$$

Unlike the coefficient of linear regression, β in Equation [10.I], and its estimate from data, r is a symmetric property of x and y. It tells nothing of whether the trend in a diagram such as Figure 10.1 is steep or shallow, but it does describe the closeness of concentration about a straight line. Whatever the values of x and y, r must lie between − 1 and + 1; $r = +1$ is possible only if all (x, y) points lie perfectly on an upward sloping straight line, $r = -1$ only if they lie on a downward sloping line. The correlation coefficient has a somewhat restricted usefulness for characterizing closeness of association; r^2 measures the amount of the total variation in y (or x) that can be explained by association with variation in x (or y), so that $r = 0.7$ corresponds to about half the variation being common to x and y. Only $r > 0.9$ (or $r < -0.9$) can reasonably be termed 'very close correlation'. The correlation coefficient can be very misleading in the presence of non-linear trends, such as that of Figure 10.4, for one can have r very close to zero even though inspection shows the points to lie almost perfectly on a smooth curve.

10.3 **Computers**

All applications of statistical methods to biological data involve graphical or arithmetical work, often very extensive calculations even for a relatively small collection of data. At one time this was a serious obstacle to good statistical analysis, because few biologists were willing to spend a great amount of time on arithmetic or on trying alternative graphical representations. The examples I have presented in earlier chapters have been kept small and simple for easy illustration of methods. Real scientific data can be as simple, but often they are far more numerous. Typically an experiment may produce measurements on 50–100 plants, animals, or other units, with perhaps two or five or more different characters measured on each. Autoanalysers, electronic monitoring equipment, and other special recording apparatus may give thousands of observations in a single study. In consequence, various quick methods were developed with the object of extracting as much information as possible from the data after minimal computational effort; tests of significance have been devised that involve little more effort than counting and comparing with standard tables, but estimation is usually more tedious.

Fortunately technical developments of electronic calculators and computers have put good computation within the reach of every scientist. Reliable pocket calculators now compare in price with textbooks. No student can regard himself as adequately equipped for courses in science if he lacks even the simple type of calculator costing up to about £10. For under £25, a range of possibilities includes direct availability of various standard functions (logarithms, exponentials, sines), programs for some common statistical calculations, and even the writing of special programs. For £50–100, calculators are available that can handle long computational sequences in a tenth of the time that would have been needed a few years ago. Nevertheless, these calculators are not suitable when large amounts of data must be analysed; for more than 100 observations, the entry of the data is tedious and the inevitable errors of key manipulation cause trouble. Most universities and scientific institutions have access to computers with far greater potential for data storage and speed of analysis, including the capacity for various types of graphical output. When observations are numbered in hundreds or when a wide range of different analyses must be performed, the computer is essential. It requires a *program*, a sequence of instructions for reading and storing the data from punched cards or other media, performing the required arithmetical operations, and outputting all the tables, lists, and diagrams that the user wants. For many types of analysis (notably analysis of variance, regression, and related matters) standard programs exist in general forms that can be applied to particular data merely by following simple instructions exactly. The BMD programs are one group that has proved useful and popular; the GENSTAT system gives much greater flexibility at a price of more complication for the user. For more complex problems, or even for apparently simple ones in which unexpected features (such as the loss of some data or lack of homogeneity of variance) are encountered, the scientist may need to write his own program. The basic rules for this, in a computer language such as FORTRAN, are easily acquired but skill demands experience that is gained only through practice and frustrating mistakes.

Although the so-called 'canned' programs, carefully written to cover a general class of analysis and with good instructions on use, may be used very effectively, the scientist who employs one in almost complete ignorance of the underlying statistical principles risks producing a lot of nonsense. Never forget that a computer is a very obedient moron. If told to analyse data in an inappropriate manner, it will do so unhesitatingly unless the form of the data makes this impossible. Some such programs are bad because of identifiable computational weaknesses. Others, including one or two that are widely used, bring more insidious dangers because their simplicity and clear presentation encourage biologists to use statistical techniques unsuitable for the problem in hand or even of questionable theoretical soundness. Yet others are excellent precision tools that still, like those of an engineer, can be misused.

Computers have removed the burden of statistical arithmetic, but they leave the user responsible for choosing the appropriate form of analysis. This warning is even more relevant to anyone who writes his own program. Having been told to start something, the computer also needs to be told when to stop; a program must contain instructions for dealing with every contingency, including such things as a divisor becoming zero or a number to be square-rooted becoming negative; if data are not to be carefully scanned by an intelligent human before submission to the computer, the program must contain instructions for handling every possible anomaly – the plant with 0 leaves, the animal for which the fourth of six weekly weighings was forgotten, the copying error that appears as an air temperature of 250° C or a litter of 88 mice. Computer users must also beware of producing so much output that they can never read it all, or of calling for so many supplementary analyses that they obscure the most important features of their data.

Every computer user continually relearns these lessons. All thought is inserted by the programmer and the user. The computer obeys; it cannot infer that the user would be better pleased if an instruction were interpreted as intended instead of as written. Indeed, one educational gain from program writing is that we learn how to express ourselves unambiguously through a long chain of instructions. If anyone doubts the difficulty of this, let him try to write instructions of equal exactness on how to wash his face or how to move from his breakfast table to his place of daily work! The contrast with the human mind is important. Often inefficient, unreliable, and slow in complicated routine tasks, you and I possess much greater potential for rapid recognition of a pattern, for being triggered by associations, and for the intuition that is the foundation of discovery.

On the other hand, the computer is almost entirely free from arithmetical mistakes of the kind that we all make when we rely on pen-and-paper arithmetic. The computer never says '$7 \times 9 = 56$'! Or rather, if a fault in the hardware does affect the arithmetical processes, this is evident because of consequences so gross and widespread as to produce a great amount of obvious nonsense in the output. If the output from a program appears to be wrong, in the absence of any warning of a major computer malfunction, the first suspicions should always be that data have been erroneously entered (e.g. a shift of a decimal point), that the instructions for operating the program have not been followed to the last detail, or that the program contains an erroneous instruction. Although one can safely assume that the required numerical steps have been performed, numerical accuracy is not always very high. Unless special devices are invoked (such as 'double length arithmetic'), individual calculations may be executed only to 5 or 6 digit accuracy, and the result of a chain of calculations may be correct only to the first 4 digits. Indeed far worse things may occur. A subtraction perhaps ought to be (14 632.451 92– 14 632.447 16) but this may be treated as (14 632.5– 14 632.4), giving the answer 0.100 00 instead of 0.004 76. Good programming minimizes these dangers; good use of a program also calls for care, so as to avoid the conjunction of quantities that may cause extreme loss of accuracy. In these matters, important differences exist between different models of computer and expert advice should be sought on all critical questions.

10.4* Multivariate analysis

Section 10.2 introduced the notion of two or more distinct variates being measured on each unit under study. Section 10.3 mentioned more elaborate possibilities of the same kind. It is indeed characteristic of quantitative biology that many measurements are made on every culture or cell or plant or community. Several forms of multivariate analysis are widely used. The commonest, most important, and logically simplest is regression with one or more independent variates. Except for simple linear regression, all multivariate analysis has great logical complexity and much is computationally expensive. This is no place for more than the briefest introduction. *Discriminant analysis* uses measurements of individuals from two or more groups, such as separate races within a species, and determines from them a linear function or other compound of the measurements that best distinguishes one group from another; this function can then be applied to new individuals for which the group is unknown and assigning each to the most likely group.

Other multivariate analyses concentrate on the internal structure of the data without reference to any external information, or external criteria of success. *Principal component analysis* and *factor analysis* attempt to express the whole variational pattern of the data in terms of a few variates compounded from those originally measured. This may achieve the object of 'reducing' the data, expressing almost all the information more concisely in fewer numerical entities. Unfortunately, there is no guarantee that the compounds will be intrinsically meaningful, or that two related sets of data will indicate recognizably similar compound variates. *Cluster analysis*, which is popular with ecologists, systematists, and students of evolution, looks for evidence that the data can be subdivided into groups with the property that members of a group are markedly more similar than members of different groups. Cluster analysis is not a single well-defined technique. There are at the present time no clear rules or criteria to guide the biologist in a choice among hundreds, perhaps thousands, of alternative sets of principles that can be used to define the numerical details. Although data that fall clearly into groups are likely to lead to qualitatively the same conclusions whatever form of cluster analysis is used, this need not be true for data that are more interesting because the pattern is less obvious. Much more research and experience is needed before cluster analysis can become a definitive statistical technique; until then all uncritical use and all implications that 'cluster analysis of these data proves . . .' should be viewed with caution and even suspicion.

10.5* Time sequences and stochastic processes

Very important in biology are measurements made at a sequence of points in time on the same organisms. These may show a steady increase, as in weekly records of weights or lengths of growing animals; they may fluctuate widely, with a nearly regular or a wholly irregular cycle, as do the numbers of animals in a natural community subject to a seasonal cycle or to changing pressures from food supplies, disease, or predators; they may fluctuate only to a small extent about a stable level, as will the heart rate or blood pressure of a hospital patient recorded every 15 minutes or on a continuous trace. The problems are diverse, but a major common feature is that successive observations are not statistically independent. A pig that is 5.0 kg below the mean for its population at 20 weeks of age cannot be 4.5 kg above the mean at 21 weeks. A colony of insects with a 2 month generation time that at the beginning of May has been reduced to very small numbers cannot be at full strength in June even though the predation has been relaxed. The statistical 'error' or deviation from the mean at any one instant is correlated with, but not completely determined by, its magnitude in the recent past. Any method of statistical analysis that ignores this type of correlation can seriously mislead. For example, data from 50 plants grown under conditions that are alike except that sets of 10 were given 8, 10, 12, 14, 16 hours of light daily could properly be subjected to analysis of variance and regression calculations. Data from 10 plants, each of which was recorded at 8, 10, 12, 14, 16 weeks after planting might be presented in a table of similar appearance but the same analysis would not apply. (This illustrates how uncritical choice of a computer program can do more harm than an intelligent attempt to assess a problem qualitatively without formal statistical techniques.)

Once again, a vast range of statistical theory and method is available. The general head of *stochastic processes* includes all situations in which the observation or measurement at one instant is stochastically (or probabilistically) dependent upon one or more of the preceding observations. In practice, analysis is excessively difficult unless the time intervals between observations are all equal. One of the simpler ideas is that of autoregression: the observations at instants 2, 3, 4, ... of time are regarded as having a linear regression on the values at instants 1, 2, 3, ..., respectively. This can be useful, but is a rather crude assumption. Many specifications more realistic for particular biological populations have been studied. For example, a population whose numbers are largely dependent upon predation cannot be discussed satisfactorily without also taking account of the numbers of the predator species; equations can be constructed to represent the manner in which each population size is governed by its own birth and death rates and by the numbers of the other species that prey upon or feed it. Theory and practice become very complicated, and none of the problems can be discussed at the level of this book. One important point to bear in mind is that the intercorrelation of data reduces the effective number of observations. An experiment on 60 rats with a single measurement on each may tell quite a lot about that one characteristic. An experiment on 3 rats each measured daily for 20 days may tell rather little about the mechanism determining the measurement, and an adequate study might need 15 rats each measured on 50 days.

Analogous methods are relevant to spatial sequences. The growth of a tree in a plantation will be affected by and will affect its neighbours. Not only are the effects now two-dimensional, but there is no distinction between 'forward' and 'backward'. The weight of a rat today cannot be affected by its weight tomorrow, but the tree is affected by its neighbours in every direction.

10.6* 'Models'

A fashionable term among biologists today is 'biological modelling'. This implies expressing all important determinants of a biological system in mathematical equations and unknown parameters, the equations often being differential equations with complicated boundary conditions. One has only to think of a system as well-defined and isolated from uncontrolled factors as the growth of a farm animal to realize the many relations that must be taken into account. The diet has constituents with different functions handled by different metabolic routes. Some aspects of growth are limited by others. Genetic factors may be important; efficiencies of conversion from chemical materials in the diet to those utilizable by the animals may be critically important, yet neither known nor estimable from observations that can be made.

Our understanding of physical sciences has grown by way of analogous mathematical specifications of reality, with alternations of experiment and improvement in the mathematics. We must hope for successful development in the vastly more complex biological sciences. We must also beware of too ready an acceptance that something described as a model is inherently better than or even logically different from such standard statistical techniques as regression. Too often 'modelling' is regarded as an excuse for guessing numerical values of troublesome parameters such as transfer and conversion rates, where a more classical statistical approach would demand that the problem of estimating them be explicitly faced.

I admit to scepticism on modelling because the ideas are so easily abused. The name itself contains dangers. To some, the temptation is that of modelling in clay – forming fragile representations of reality, aesthetically pleasing but containing too many uncertainties to be a contribution to the understanding of truth. To others, the temptation is that of play with model engines – the fascination of working with a small scale and easily controlled representation can induce an enthusiasm for the model that displaces concern for reality. But scepticism is not enough. Biology must eventually progress in this way; quantitative genetics, and plant and animal breeding have already done so, other branches must follow. The road is difficult, and the sceptic has a place in restraining facile over-confidence, but for the next century at least there will be vast scope for adding to the completeness of mathematical specification of how biological systems behave.

10.7 Final advice

If you have understood most of these ten chapters, you now have a basic knowledge of the principles and objectives of statistical science. I have not tried to teach you to do much for yourself. Even practical classes in quantitative biology, and certainly any type of research, will rapidly take you to the limits of the simple methods I have illustrated and will require you to learn how to use more complex techniques. There are many books that can help you. There are also books that will harm more than help; an easy style of presentation is not a guarantee that the author is a safe guide, and you should take advice from an experienced biometrician or statistician on a book suited to your needs. Among those that can help without demanding any great amount of mathematical theory, I suggest (in ascending order of difficulty):

P. SPRENT (1977) *Statistics in Action* (Penguin Books, Harmondsworth, Middlesex)

R. E. PARKER (1973) *Introductory Statistics for Biology* (Edward Arnold Ltd, London)

N. GILBERT (1973) *Biometrical Interpretation* (Clarendon Press, Oxford)

D. J. FINNEY (1972) *An Introduction to Statistical Science in Agriculture* (Munksgaard, Copenhagen)

G. W. SNEDECOR and W. G. COCHRAN (1967) *Statistical Methods* (Iowa State University Press, Ames, Iowa, USA)

D. R. COX (1958) *Planning of Experiments* (John Wiley & Sons, New York)

D. COLQUHOUN (1971) *Lectures in Biostatistics* (Clarendon Press, Oxford)

R. R. SOKAL and F. J. ROHLF (1973) *Introduction to Biostatistics* (W. H. Freeman & Co., San Francisco, USA)

These books are all introductory, though some provide good basic instruction in the use of statistical methods. A biologist wishing to make effective use of the ideas mentioned in this chapter will almost certainly need either much discussion with a statistician or study of more advanced texts.

If you are to undertake a biological investigation involving any form of numerical assessment, you should think of statistical aspects at an early stage of your planning. Choice of a design needs consideration over a long time rather than in a single concentrated effort. Unless you are very sure that you know what you should do, consult a statistician. You need to be clear why you are investigating and what information you want to obtain. Keep very full records of everything you do, being particularly careful about all numerical information. Remember that you personally are fallible in all your arithmetic and in any copying of numbers; so am I, and so is most of humanity, but what matters to *you* is the time that *you* say 7×8 is 63 or copy 337.46 as 377.46. Always scan your data thoughtfully before beginning any statistical analysis: you will often find that some pattern becomes apparent, some copying error is recognized, or some anomaly shouts at you. But do not reject a value merely because it looks extraordinary; use it instead as a warning that you should check all your records and earlier computations for any explanation.

In numerical examples in earlier chapters, I have tried to display good arrangements of calculations, but my illustrations are on a very small scale. You must cultivate good habits of setting out every step of an analysis clearly for future reference. Avoid scraps of paper. Any value that needs to be written should have its place in your records. Use paper generously, and write in ink, never pencil. When you report on results, use simple tables and diagrams clearly labelled. A large table, or a diagram with many points and curves ensures that few will understand it. Your conclusions should be written in language appropriate to your subject matter, not in a mass of statistical jargon that you have not yourself fully digested.

Statistical science is a great aid to biological research and understanding. It is not an end in itself. If your statistical analysis appears to be telling a story markedly different from what the original data suggest to you, be sceptical about the analysis. Have you used an inappropriate method or made a gross mistake? Of course you should aim to explain and remove any conflict of interpretation, but in doing so never forget that good data from good biological investigations are of first importance, and statistical analyses exist solely for extracting and refining the truth from the data.

Solutions to exercises

Many solutions are presented only in outline; where novel points arise I give details.

Chapter 1

1.1 Successive classes from 156 to 194 have frequencies
2, 0, 0, 1, 0, 1, 1, 2, 3, 4, 3, 6, 3, 7, 7, 6, 5, 11, 7, 2
3, 5, 6, 9, 11, 4, 5, 7, 7, 3, 5, 2, 6, 0, 2, 1, 1, 1, 1;
all others have frequency 0.

1.2 Results are obtained by simple additions from Exercise 1.1; for example,

156 – 160	161 – 165	166 – 170	171 – 175	176 – 180
3	11	26	31	34

181 – 185	186 – 190	191 – 195	Total
26	15	4	150

Groups in Exercise 1.1 are so narrow that frequencies are low and pattern is irregular. Groups of 10 cm width are so coarse that they suppress most of information.

1.3 Histogram shows observed frequency of observations within an interval as rectangular block of area proportional to frequency. Those for Exercises 1.1 and 1.2 are

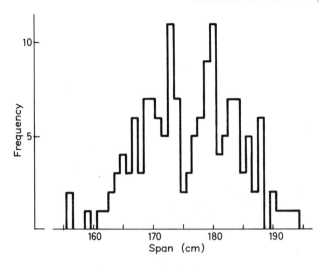

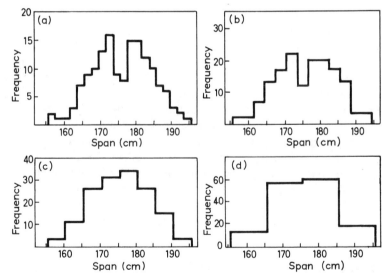

1.4 There are $2^4 = 16$ possible sequences. List systematically as HHHH, HHHT, HHTH, HHTT, HTHH, HTHT, ... Then by counting

No. of H/T	4/0	3/1	2/2	1/3	0/4
Frequency	1	4	6	4	1

Note that frequencies of the numbers of heads are binomial

coefficients from expansion

$$(1 + a)^4 = 1 + 4a + 6a^2 + 4a^3 + a^4.$$

Number of sequences	Probability
(i) 6	$6/16 = 3/8$
(ii) 5 ($= 1 + 4$)	$5/16$
(iii) 5	$5/16$
(iv) 0 (impossible)	0
(v) 4	$4/16 = 1/4$

If bias made H relatively more probable than T, probability of (ii) would obviously increase and that of (iii) would decrease; (iv) would remain impossible. Effects on (i) and (v) cannot be discussed without Section 4.3. General probability for (i), $6P^2(1 - P)^2$, has maximum at $P = \frac{1}{2}$ and therefore is decreased by any bias. General probability for (v), $4P^3(1 - P)$, increases with P up to $P = 3/4$ and then decreases again as probability of heads approaches certainty.

1.5 Three events (i) H, (ii) TH, (iii) TT are not equally likely; (i) includes two possible sequences (ia) HH, (ib) HT. Four events (ia), (ib), (ii), (iii) are made equally likely by spinning fair coin. Each has probability $\frac{1}{4}$, three include H at least once, and required probability is therefore 3/4.

1.6 Obtaining data on drug consumption in any other way may be difficult, but must be recognized that response is likely to be poor, those who have taken the drug may not always know the name, memory over 5 years can be unreliable, those who have not taken the drug are perhaps least likely and those who have taken large quantities most likely to respond to the inquiry. Consequently a mean dose for those who respond may seriously overestimate the mean of the whole community.

Chapter 2

2.1 170.4, 181.4, 174.2, 174.6. Frequencies

165.5–170.5	170.5–175.5	175.5–180.5	180.5–185.5	Total
3	11	11	5	30

are much more concentrated towards centre than were those in Exercise 1.2.

2.2 If same scale were used throughout, total area would decline from 5000 to 100 units. Interesting feature is relative shape, which, as in Exercises 1.2 and 2.1, would become steadily more concentrated towards centre, i.e. *relatively* narrower and taller. Theory (Chapter 6) shows relevant factor to be square root of number of individuals: 200 means of 25 will have a histogram about $1/\sqrt{25} = 1/5$ width of that of original observations, but heights of rectangles will be increased by a compensating factor in order to keep total areas comparable. Biologist studying mouse weights is interested in mean of conceptually large population, not in single mouse. By using instead mean of 30, he obtains a value of type more closely concentrated about population mean than if he based his study on single mouse.

2.3 Discussion of any of these could be lengthy.

(i) Assign a number to each name on a membership list. Select 100 by a lottery, either actual drawing of numbered tickets or with table of random numbers. There will be difficulties if list is not up to date. Conference sample may be biased against those who live at great distance, who are too elderly to attend, or whose status does not allow them to leave work in time to arrive for first social gathering. In sampling human populations, individual behaviour patterns may be very important.

(ii) Method mentioned is likely to be used in practice; draining body and sampling from total blood content has little practical appeal. We need to ask whether blood is well mixed within body and whether any types of abnormal cells might be less or more likely to come out from a small puncture. Would 8 hours sleep or 10 minutes vigorous exercise before sampling affect things? I do not know; I should want to talk with a physiologist before giving definitive statistical advice.

(iii) Small seeds can be sampled much as a liquid. For example, stir and mix whole bulk by hand and discard approximately half. Then mix again and discard half, repeating until rather more than 100 remain. Arrange these in a line, number them, and draw lots. Last step may be important, as any subjective process might permit subconscious preference for larger seeds or conscious rejection of damaged or discoloured seeds. Spoon could be useful first step if bag is well mixed (e.g. no tendency for smallest to have sunk to the bottom); process described is safer than merely counting first 100 from spoon.

(iv) Scheme suggested could give good sample of *usage* rather than *users*; well spread over times of day and days of week, but biased in favour of frequent users. About only way of taking sample of users is to draw lots from list of those authorized. For library that has no such list, sampling would be very difficult.

2.4

	Mathematics	No mathematics	Total
Men	90	510	600
Women	40	360	400
Total	130	870	1000

(i) $130/1000 = 0.13$; (ii) $40/130 = 0.31$.

Chapter 3

3.1 36 possibilities, each with probability $1/36$, correspond with cells of following table:

Die A

Die B	1	2	3	4	5	6
1		×		×		×
2	×		×		×	
3		×		×		×
4	×		×		×	
5		×		×		×
6	×		×		×	

(i) Count 25 cells in which neither die shows '2':

$$Pr(\text{no } 2) = 25/36.$$

(ii) Diagonal cells are only ones with equal scores:

$$Pr(\text{equal scores}) = 6/36 = 1/6.$$

(iii) Only perfect squares that can be formed are 4 and 9, first in 3 ways $(3 + 1, 2 + 2, 1 + 3)$ and second in 4:

$$Pr(\text{total is square}) = 7/36.$$

(iv) Cells marked are those for which difference is ± 1, ± 3, ± 5:

$$Pr(\text{odd difference}) = 18/36 = 1/2.$$

3.2

	White	Red	Total
A	8	12	20
B	42	28	70
Total	50	40	90

(i) Relative frequency of red is 0.6 for A, 0.4 for B. Coin ensures that each has probability 1/2 of being applicable:

$$Pr(\text{red}) = \frac{1}{2} \times 0.6 + \frac{1}{2} \times 0.4 = 0.5.$$

(ii) From bottom of table:

$$Pr(\text{red}) = 40/90 = 0.44.$$

3.3

	Blood test	None	Total
Men	9%	51%	60%
Women	4%	36%	40%
Total	13%	87%	100%

(i) $13/100 = 0.13$;   (ii) $4/13 = 0.31$.

3.4

	Infested	Clean	Proportion
Q.r.	$0.7 \times 0.05 = 0.035$	0.665	0.7
Q.p.	$0.3 \times 0.2 = 0.060$	0.240	0.3
Total	0.095	0.905	1.0

(i) 0.095;   (ii) $0.060/0.095 = 0.63$.

3.5 Information can be summarized

	Probability of classification by quick test		
Truth	G (good)	D (doubtful)	B (bad)
G	0.75	0.20	0.05
B	0.10	0.10	0.80

(i) Probability that a bad piece is used $= 0.2$. Since each such piece wastes 200 minutes, expected cost in time $= 0.2 \times 200 = 40$ minutes per piece.

(ii) Every piece costs 10 minutes of testing time.

(iii) (a) Every piece costs 1 minute for Test B;

(b) Of all pieces, probability that Test B says 'doubtful' $= 0.8 \times 0.20 + 0.2 \times 0.10 = 0.18$,
and expectation of time for Test A on these $= 0.18 \times 10 = 1.8$ minutes;

(c) Expectation of waste from good pieces being classed as bad and rejected $= 0.8 \times 0.05 \times 20 = 0.8$ minutes;

(d) Expectation of waste from attempt to use bad pieces classed as good $= 0.2 \times 0.10 \times 200 = 4.0$ minutes.

Hence total cost in time $= 1 + 1.8 + 0.8 + 4.0$
$= 7.6$ minutes.

Clearly omission of all testing would be foolish, and the adoption of the complicated scheme (iii) will on average save 2.4 minutes per piece, or almost one-quarter of the testing time required for (ii).

3.6 Remove any components capable of showing a positive result! 'New' machine will classify 900 correctly:

	Machine record		
	−	+	Total
Diseased	100	0	100
Healthy	900	0	900

3.7 As in Exercise 3.3, form the table of probabilities in the population.

	Test −	Test +	
Diseased	0.04	0.16	0.2
Healthy	0.72	0.08	0.8
	0.76	0.24	1.00

of the proportion of the population that give a positive test result, 0.16/0.24 or 2/3 are diseased. Also the probability that a diseased cow remains diseased after drug treatment is 0.3; since healthy cows remain healthy after treatment, the probability that a treated cow remains diseased is therefore

$$(0.3 \times 0.16)/0.24 = 0.2.$$

Chapter 4

4.1 Flowers on a plant will be all red or all white and gardener is likely to have grown rows of one colour; therefore successive flowers picked are not independent. For instance, he might have 20 rows of red and 60 rows of white plants; if varieties flower equally freely, $P = \frac{1}{4}$ for randomly chosen bloom. Gardener picks from one row only. If he starts in random row, $Pr(50 \text{ red}) = \frac{1}{4}$, $Pr(50 \text{ white}) = \frac{3}{4}$, Pr (bunch of mixed colours) = 0. Beware of binomial when it is not applicable!

4.2 Either 5 or 6 'sixes':

$$\text{Probability} = 6P^5(1 - P) + P^6.$$

4.3 Must have 28 or more ewes with twins:

$$\text{Probability} = \sum_{r = 28}^{r = 55} \begin{bmatrix} 55 \\ r \end{bmatrix} P^r(1 - P)^{55 - r}.$$

4.4 Most people (not the author!) have two eyes of same colour. Consequently 20 eyes of 10 men consist of 10 non-independent pairs. Binomial distribution is not applicable. Suppose you were asked similar question about hair colour − say grey hair, with $P = 0.15$ − a sample of 10 men and 50 hairs taken from each head. Any application of binomial (for eyes or hair) must be to 10 men, not to 20 eyes or 500 hairs.

4.5 He needs to have 1 or 3 or 5 red books:

$$\text{Probability} = 5P(1 - P)^4 + 10P^3(1 - P)^2 + P^5.$$

4.6 Proportions are (complete table in order of numbers in parentheses):

	Test negative	Test positive	Proportion
Diseased	0.001 (5)	0.009 (4)	0.01 (2)
Healthy	0.792 (7)	0.198 (6)	0.99 (3)
Total	0.793 (9)	0.207 (8)	1.00 (1)

Probability that animal with positive test is diseased = $0.0009/0.207 = 0.043$.

If investigator classes animal as diseased only when two independent tests are both positive,

$$Pr \text{(class as diseased)} = (0.9)^2 \text{ for diseased animal,}$$
$$= (0.2)^2 \text{ for healthy animal.}$$

Similar calculations lead to probability = $0.0081/0.0477 = 0.17$.

4.7 (i) Distinguish females as A and B. Possible numbers of daughters and associated probabilities are:

A	B	$5^2 \times$ Probability
0	1	$1 \times 3 = 3$
0	2	$1 \times 1 = 1$
1	0	$3 \times 1 = 3$
1	1	$3 \times 3 = 9$
1	2	$3 \times 1 = 3$
2	0	$1 \times 1 = 1$
2	1	$1 \times 3 = 3$
2	2	$1 \times 1 = 1$
		Total = 24

Each line comes from combination of independent probabilities:

$$Pr \text{(A has 0 and B has 1)} = Pr \text{(A has 0)} \times Pr \text{(B has 1)}$$

$$= \frac{1}{5} \times \frac{3}{5} = 3/5^2.$$

The eight possibilities are mutually exclusive, and total probability is 24/25. Alternatively, note that only possibility *not* giving at least 1 daughter is that neither female produces a daughter. Probability $= (1/5)(1/5) = 1/25$. Probability of 1 or more daughters is the complement, $1 - 1/25$.

(ii) Tabulate systematically ways of producing exactly 3 daughters:

A	B	C	$5^3 \times$ Probability
0	1	2	$1 \times 3 \times 1 = 3$
0	2	1	$1 \times 1 \times 3 = 3$
1	0	2	$3 \times 1 \times 1 = 3$
1	1	1	$3 \times 3 \times 3 = 27$
1	2	0	$3 \times 1 \times 1 = 3$
2	0	1	$1 \times 1 \times 3 = 3$
2	1	0	$1 \times 3 \times 1 = 3$
			Total $= 45$

Total probability $= 45/125 = 9/25$. No shorter solution exists.

(iii) Ways of obtaining at least one granddaughter are:

1 daughter who does *not* have 0 daughters,

2 daughters, and *not* both of these fail to have daughters.

$$\text{Total probability} = \frac{3}{5} \times \left(1 - \frac{1}{5}\right) + \frac{1}{5} \times \left[1 - \left(\frac{1}{5}\right)^2\right]$$
$$= \frac{12}{25} + \frac{24}{125} = 84/125.$$

4.8

	Normal	Abnormal	Total
Before	72	8	80
After	87	33	120
Total	159	41	200

From final line, proportion abnormal is:

$$41/200 = 0.205.$$

As in Section 3.6, expected frequency of abnormals before drug is:

$$80 \times 0.205 = 16.4.$$

Table of expectations is:

	Normal	Abnormal	Total
Before	63.6	16.4	80
After	95.4	24.6	120
Total	159	41	200

Hence values of 'O − E' are:

$$\begin{matrix} 8.4 & -8.4 \\ -8.4 & 8.4. \end{matrix}$$

Therefore

$$\chi^2 = \frac{7.9^2}{63.6} + \frac{7.9^2}{16.4} + \frac{7.9^2}{95.4} + \frac{7.9^2}{24.6}$$
$$= 0.98 + 3.81 + 0.65 + 2.54$$
$$= 7.98.$$

This is much greater than 3.84; null hypothesis that proportion of abnormal cells is same before and after administration of the drug is rejected because of clear evidence that proportion of abnormals has increased.

Must not conclude that 'drug increases abnormal cells in cats', only that there has been an increase in *this* cat. Perhaps in this cat increase would have taken place without drug. A proper experiment would sample a population of cats and compare several cats with drug and several cats similarly treated but not having drug.

4.9   For option (i), expectation of number of doubles is $16 \times \frac{1}{2} = 8$. Probability of at least 5 requires summation of binomial probabilities for $5, 6, 7, \ldots, 16$:

$$P_1 = \binom{16}{5}\left(\frac{1}{2}\right)^5\left(\frac{1}{2}\right)^{11} + \binom{16}{6}\left(\frac{1}{2}\right)^6\left(\frac{1}{2}\right)^{10}$$
$$+ \binom{16}{7}\left(\frac{1}{2}\right)^7\left(\frac{1}{2}\right)^9 + \ldots + \left(\frac{1}{2}\right)^{16}.$$

For option (ii), probability of survival of any seedling is

$$1 - \frac{1}{3} = \frac{2}{3}.$$

Probability that a seedling is double and survives $= \frac{2}{3} \times \frac{1}{2} = \frac{1}{3}$.
Expectation of doubles that survive $= 24 \times \frac{1}{3} = 8$ again.
Required probability now requires summation for 5, 6,
7, . . . , 24:

$$P_2 = \binom{24}{5}\left(\frac{1}{3}\right)^5\left(\frac{2}{3}\right)^{19} + \binom{24}{6}\left(\frac{1}{3}\right)^6\left(\frac{2}{3}\right)^{18} + \ldots + \left(\frac{1}{3}\right)^{24}.$$

If plant breeder is equally content with either option on all
grounds other than success (e.g. they are equally troublesome or
equally costly to him), he should choose higher value of P. If he
prefers one option on grounds of convenience or expense, he
should consider whether any greater value of P for other can
counterbalance his preference. Arithmetic shows that $P_1 =$
0.962 and $P_2 = 0.941$; both are good, but (ii) is appreciably
more likely to fail than (i). To shorten arithmetic, find complementary probabilities $(1 - P_1)$, $(1 - P_2)$, these being probabilities of failure to obtain 5 doubles. Thus:

$$1 - P_2 = \left(\frac{2}{3}\right)^{24} + 24\left(\frac{1}{3}\right)\left(\frac{2}{3}\right)^{23} + \binom{24}{2}\left(\frac{1}{3}\right)^2\left(\frac{2}{3}\right)^{22} + \ldots$$
$$+ \binom{24}{4}\left(\frac{1}{3}\right)^4\left(\frac{2}{3}\right)^{20}.$$

4.10 For all plants, proportion of smooth leaved is

$$108/480 = 0.225.$$

Hence obtain expectations:

Leaf	Dark blue	Light blue	Yellow	Pink	White	Total
Rough	34.100	93.000	41.850	51.925	151.125	372
Smooth	9.900	27.000	12.150	15.075	43.875	108
Total	44	120	54	67	195	480

This strongly suggests that blue smooths are scarcer than
general average of smooths suggests, yellows and pinks more
common. Calculated as in Section 4.5, $\chi^2 = 31.0$, so large as
scarcely to require reference to Table 4.1. The NH, colour and
leaf type are independent, is firmly rejected.

4.11 Null hypothesis should be: 'of subjects who succeed with only
one hand, that hand is equally likely to be right or left.' Hence

(30 + 13) observations from binomial distribution with

$$Pr\,(\text{right}) = \frac{1}{2}.$$

As in Section 4.4,

	Right	Left	Total
Observed	30	13	43
Expected	21.5	21.5	43

Hence

$$\chi^2 = \frac{(8.5 - 0.5)^2}{21.5} + \frac{(8.5 - 0.5)^2}{21.5} = 2.98 + 2.98 = 5.96.$$

This exceeds 3.84. Reject null hypothesis because, if it were true, data tell us that event with probability less than 0.05 has occurred; there is considerable evidence that success with right hand is more likely than success with left. To estimate success rates, need also to know numbers who succeed with right and with left, but this is irrelevant to test of significance.

4.12   (i) Random selection ensures independence of successive plants. Hence probability is

$$\frac{1}{4} \times \frac{1}{4} \times \frac{1}{4} \times \frac{1}{2} = 1/128.$$

(ii) Probability of non-pink is $\frac{1}{2}$. Required probability is obtained from binomial distribution as

$$\binom{4}{2}\left(\frac{1}{2}\right)^2\left(\frac{1}{2}\right)^2 = 3/8.$$

(iii) $\binom{4}{2}\left(\frac{1}{2}\right)^2\left(\frac{1}{2}\right)^2 + \binom{4}{3}\left(\frac{1}{2}\right)\left(\frac{1}{2}\right)^3 + \left(\frac{1}{2}\right)^4 = 11/16.$

Probability of n white in n trials $= (\frac{1}{4})^n$. For $n = 5$, this is $1/1024$, and therefore probability of at least one one white $= 1023/1024$.

4.13 As in Section 4.3,

Probability of 3 or less

$$= \left(\frac{3}{4}\right)^{30} + 30\left(\frac{3}{4}\right)^{29}\left(\frac{1}{4}\right) + \binom{30}{2}\left(\frac{3}{4}\right)^{28}\left(\frac{1}{4}\right)^2 + \binom{30}{3}\left(\frac{3}{4}\right)^{27}\left(\frac{1}{4}\right)^3$$

$= 0.000\ 18 + 0.001\ 78 + 0.008\ 63 + 0.002\ 685$

$= 0.037.$

Deficiency relative to expectation of 7.5 Q-cells would be judged statistically significant at probability 0.05.

Chapter 5

5.1   Because scarcely any insects are between 200 mg and 350 mg, $F(y)$ must be almost constant over this range. Constant level corresponds to proportion of males in the population, since $F(250)$, probability of a weight less than 250 mg, is essentially same thing as probability that an insect is male. Hence distribution functions will be similar to:

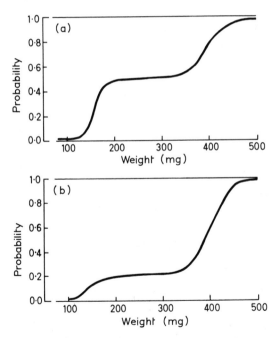

5.2   (a) Numbers in any year of age must be less than in preceding year. Curve must rise steadily from zero with slope that is always decreasing.

(b) Almost always cloud cover is very close to zero. Ordinate of distribution function must exceed 0.98 even for very small percentage cloud such as 1%.

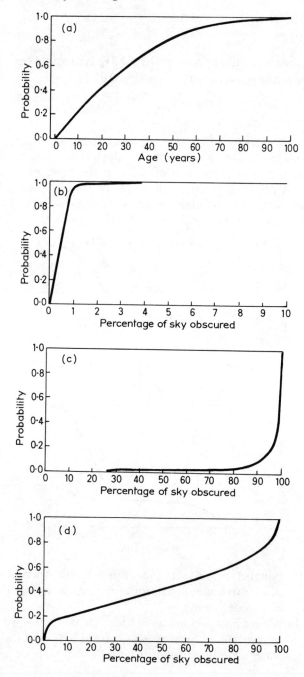

(c) Opposite of (b). Usually nearly complete cloud cover; probability of less than, say, 97% cloud must still be small.

(d) Characteristic British pattern is perhaps much more even, but with small probability of nearly clear sky, fairly large probability of almost complete cover, and between say 10% and 80% cover steady increase in distribution function.

(e) You guess! Possibly small proportion have practically no athletic activity, larger proportion of enthusiasts play or train for 12 hours a week or more, and remainder are fairly uniformly distributed between. Outcome would be a curve similar to (d).

5.3
$$(y_i - d)^2 = (y_i - \bar{y})^2 + 2(\bar{y} - d)(y_i - \bar{y}) + (\bar{y} - d)^2.$$

Hence

$$\sum (y_i - d)^2 = \sum (y_i - \bar{y})^2 + 2(\bar{y} - d)\sum (y_i - \bar{y}) + n(\bar{y} - d)^2;$$

$(\bar{y} - d)$ is constant for all members of sample and can be taken outside any summation. Also

$$\sum (y_i - \bar{y}) = \sum y_i - n\bar{y} = 0$$

by definition of $\bar{y}$. Consequently

$$\sum (y_i - d)^2 = \sum (y_i - \bar{y})^2 + (n\bar{y} - nd)^2/n$$
$$= \sum (y_i - \bar{y})^2 + (\sum y_i - nd)^2/n.$$

If we put $d = 0$, we can write

$$\sum (y_i - \bar{y})^2 = \sum y_i^2 - (\sum y_i)^2/n, \qquad \text{[5.IX]}$$

an exceedingly important standard form of calculation for arithmetical simplicity. Another formula, not proved here but especially useful with a computer is

$$\sum (y_i - \bar{y})^2 = \frac{(y_2 - y_1)^2}{1 \times 2} + \frac{(2y_3 - y_1 - y_2)^2}{2 \times 3}$$
$$+ \frac{(3y_4 - y_1 - y_2 - y_3)^2}{3 \times 4} + \dots$$

where right-hand side continues in obvious manner for $(n - 1)$ terms.

Since all squares of numbers are positive, formula in this exercise proves

$$\sum (y_i - \bar{y})^2 < \sum (y_i - d)^2$$

unless $d = \bar{y}$. Hence, unless sample happens to have $\bar{y} = \mu$ exactly,

$$\sum (y_i - \bar{y})^2 < \sum (y_i - \mu)^2.$$

Because

$$\sum (y_i - \mu)^2/n$$

is certainly unbiased estimator of mean square deviation σ^2,

$$\sum (y_i - \bar{y})^2/n$$

must be biased (Section 5.7). Fortunately easy adjustment leads to unbiased estimator s^2.

5.4   From

$$y_i = \mu + (y_i - \mu),$$

$$E(y_i^2) = \mu^2 + 2\mu E(y_i - \mu) + E[(y_i - \mu)^2] = \mu^2 + 0 + \sigma^2.$$

Similarly, if $i \neq j$,

$$E(y_i y_j) = \mu^2 + \mu E(y_i - \mu) + \mu E(y_j - \mu) + E[(y_i - \mu)(y_j - \mu)]$$
$$= \mu^2.$$

5.5   From Exercise 5.4,

$$E[(\sum y_i)^2] = nE(y_i^2) + n(n-1)E(y_i y_j)$$
$$= n\mu^2 + n\sigma^2 + n(n-1)\mu^2.$$

Using Equations [5.IX] and [5.XIII],

$$E[\sum (y_i - \bar{y})^2] = n\mu^2 + n\sigma^2 - \mu^2 - \sigma^2 - (n-1)\mu^2$$
$$= (n-1)\sigma^2.$$

This proves that s^2 in Equation [5.VIII] is an unbiased estimator of σ^2

Chapter 6

6.1   For girls

$$t = \frac{86.0 - \mu}{\sqrt{(225.0/9)}}$$
$$= (86.0 - \mu)/5.0.$$

If $G(A) = 0.95$, $A = 1.96$, and as in Equation [6.IV] limits are

$$\mu_L = 86.0 - 5.0 \times 1.96 = 76.2,$$
$$h_U = 86.0 + 5.0 \times 1.96 = 95.8.$$

Verify that any value of μ between 76.2 and 95.8 will satisfy inequality on t for probability 0.95. For limits at probability 0.99, tabular value 2.58 must replace 1.96; limits are 73.1, 98.9. Calculations for boys require variance of $\bar{y}$ to be $225.0/25 = 9.0$. Limits at probability 0.95 are 78.1, 89.9 and at 0.99 they are 76.3, 91.7.

6.2   Interval on either side of $\bar{y}$ will be less than 2.0 only if number tested, n, satisfies

$$\sqrt{(225.0/n)} \times 2.58 < 2.0$$
$$\text{or} \quad 15.0 \times 2.58 < 2.0\sqrt{n}$$
$$\text{or} \quad 374.4 < n.$$

At least 375 girls and 375 boys are needed.

6.3   For Series D

$$\sum(y_i - \bar{y})^2 = (14 - 12)^2 + (8 - 12)^2 + (3 - 12)^2 + (20 - 12)^2$$
$$+ (18 - 12)^2 + (9 - 12)^2 + (12 - 12)^2$$
$$= 4 + 16 + 81 + 64 + 36 + 9 + 0$$
$$= 210.$$

Using Equation [5.IX]

$$14^2 + 8^2 + 3^2 + 20^2 + 18^2 + 9^2 + 12^2 - 84^2/7 = 1218 - 1008$$
$$= 210.$$

We shall want these two results again in Section 9.6. For Series E, result is 50 and for Section 5.7 results are 8 and 1946.

6.4   Direct calculation from deviations is easy in Exercise 6.3, because each $\bar{y}$ is an integer. Here arithmetic is less simple. For $n = 3$

$$\sum(y_i - \bar{y})^2 = (1 - 3.33)^2 + (4 - 3.33)^2 + (5 - 3.33)^2 = 8.67,$$

and using Equation [5.IX]

$$\sum(y_i - \bar{y})^2 = 1^2 + 4^2 + 5^2 - 10^2/3 = 42 - 33.33 = 8.67.$$

Results for $n = 2$, $n = 4$ are 4.50, 60.75, respectively. Third possibility is best looked at first for $n = 4$:

$$\sum(y_i - \bar{y})^2 = \frac{(4 - 1)^2}{2} + \frac{(2 \times 5 - 1 - 4)^2}{6}$$
$$+ \frac{(-3 \times 5 - 1 - 4 - 5)^2}{12}$$
$$= 4.50 + 4.17 + 52.08 = 60.75.$$

The first term and first two terms give other two results.

6.5

$$E[f\bar{y} + (1-f)\bar{z}] = E(f\bar{y}) + E[(1-f)\bar{z}]$$
$$= fE(\bar{y}) + (1-f)E(\bar{z})$$
$$= f\mu + (1-f)\mu = \mu,$$
$$Var[f\bar{y} + (1-f)\bar{z}] = Var(f\bar{y}) + Var[(1-f)\bar{z}]$$
$$= f^2 Var(\bar{y}) + (1-f)^2 Var(\bar{z})$$
$$= f^2 H + (1-f)^2 J.$$

Calling this last expression B,

$$dB/df = 2fH - 2(1-f)J.$$

If $dB/df = 0$, $f = J/(H+J)$. Also

$$d^2 B/df^2 = 2H + 2J > 0$$

because variances (H, J) are necessarily positive; hence B has minimum for this f. Substitution leads to $HJ/(H+J)$ as the minimum. Alternative formula allows you to avoid differentiation. Because H, J and squares of numbers are necessarily positive, neither term in that formula can be negative. Second term does not depend on f; first term has minimum value 0 with $f = J/(H+J)$. Minimum variance is therefore $HJ/(H+J)$.

6.6 Here $H = 12.0$, $J = 6.0$; optimal $f = 6/(12+6) = 1/3$, and estimate is

$$\frac{1}{3} \times 91.0 + \frac{2}{3} \times 94.0 = 93.0,$$

with variance $(12.0 \times 6.0)/(12.0 + 6.0) = 4.0$.

Chapter 7

7.1 Each face has probability 1/6 of being uppermost. Hence

$$\mu = E(y) = (1 - 2 - 2 + 3 + 3 + 3)\frac{1}{6} = 1.0,$$

and

$$\sigma^2 = Var(y) = (0^2 + 3^2 + 3^2 + 2^2 + 2^2 + 2^2)\frac{1}{6} = 5.0.$$

7.2 Body of table shows total scores and, in ( ), products of probabilities:

Throw 1

	$1 \left(\frac{1}{6}\right)$	$-2 \left(\frac{2}{6}\right)$	$3 \left(\frac{3}{6}\right)$
$1 \left(\frac{1}{6}\right)$	$2 \left(\frac{1}{36}\right)$	$-1 \left(\frac{2}{36}\right)$	$4 \left(\frac{3}{36}\right)$
Throw $-2 \left(\frac{2}{6}\right)$	$-1 \left(\frac{2}{36}\right)$	$-4 \left(\frac{4}{36}\right)$	$1 \left(\frac{6}{36}\right)$
2 $3 \left(\frac{3}{6}\right)$	$4 \left(\frac{3}{36}\right)$	$1 \left(\frac{6}{36}\right)$	$6 \left(\frac{9}{36}\right)$

Possible total scores and their probabilities are:

-4	-1	1	2	4	6
4/36	4/36	12/36	1/36	6/36	9/36

Hence

$$E(x) = (-4 \times 4 - 1 \times 4 + 1 \times 12 + 2 \times 1 + 4 \times 6 + 6 \times 9)/36$$
$$= 2.0,$$

$$Var(x) = [(-6)^2 \times 4 + (-3)^2 \times 4 + (-1)^2 \times 12 + 0^2 \times 1$$
$$+ 2^2 \times 6 + 4^2 \times 9]/36 = 10.0.$$

7.3

Throw 1

	$1 \left(\frac{1}{6}\right)$	$-2 \left(\frac{2}{6}\right)$	$3 \left(\frac{3}{6}\right)$
$1 \left(\frac{1}{6}\right)$	$0 \left(\frac{1}{36}\right)$	$-3 \left(\frac{2}{36}\right)$	$2 \left(\frac{3}{36}\right)$
Throw $-2 \left(\frac{2}{6}\right)$	$3 \left(\frac{2}{36}\right)$	$0 \left(\frac{4}{36}\right)$	$5 \left(\frac{6}{36}\right)$
2 $3 \left(\frac{3}{6}\right)$	$-2 \left(\frac{3}{36}\right)$	$-5 \left(\frac{6}{36}\right)$	$0 \left(\frac{9}{36}\right)$

Possible values of v and their probabilities are:

$$-5 \quad -3 \quad -2 \quad 0 \quad 2 \quad 3 \quad 5$$

$$\frac{6}{36} \quad \frac{2}{36} \quad \frac{3}{36} \quad \frac{14}{36} \quad \frac{3}{36} \quad \frac{2}{36} \quad \frac{6}{36}$$

Hence $E(v) = 0.0$, $Var(v) = 10.0$, and

$$E(v) = E(y_1) - E(y_2),$$
$$Var(v) = Var(y_1) + Var(y_2).$$

Note particularly $+$ sign in last equation. May summarize:

$$E(y_1 + y_2) = E(y_1) + E(y_2), \qquad \text{[7.III]}$$
$$E(y_1 - y_2) = E(y_1) - E(y_2), \qquad \text{[7.IV]}$$
$$Var(y_1 + y_2) = Var(y_1) + Var(y_2), \qquad \text{[7.V]}$$
$$Var(y_1 - y_2) = Var(y_1) + Var(y_2). \qquad \text{[7.VI]}$$

Note that Equations [7.III] and [7.IV], particular cases of Equation [5.XIV], do not require distributions of y_1, y_2 to be identical. Truth of Equations [7.V] and [7.VI] depends upon y_1, y_2 being statistically independent but also does not require identical distributions.

7.4

$$Var(\bar{y}) = 500.0/20 = (5.0)^2.$$

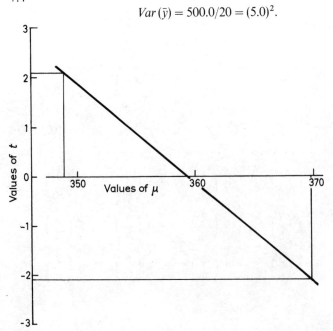

Hence
$$t_{19} = (359.4 - \mu)/5.0.$$

Several diagrammatic presentations possible. That illustrated plots value of t against μ, and shows values of μ for which t lies between -2.093, and 2.093. Rule horizontal lines at $t = 2.093$, $t = -2.093$, then verticals at their intersection with sloping line that represents t against μ. Verticals intersect axis at 348.9, 369.9, points that limit plausible values for μ.

7.5 For success with 5 plants, must have $\bar{y} \geqslant 20$. Lower limit gives
$$t = (20 - 21)/\sqrt{(6^2/5)} = -1/\sqrt{(7.2)} = -0.373.$$

Inspection of Table 6.1 suggests $A = 0.373$ would correspond to about 0.3 for $G(A)$ – sufficiently close for illustration here though more detailed table gives 0.290. By splitting range into two parts and using symmetry of whole distribution,
$$Pr(-0.373 \leqslant t) = Pr(-0.373 \leqslant t \leqslant 0) + Pr(0 \leqslant t)$$
$$= (\text{approx.}) \tfrac{1}{2} \times 0.3 + 0.5 = 0.65.$$

Biochemist has about 2 chances in 3 of success; from more exact table, probability $= 0.645$. With 6 plants, minimal $\bar{y}$ is 100/6 and
$$t = (16.67 - 21)/\sqrt{(6^2/6)} = -1.77.$$

Effect is great. Now from Table 6.1, $G(1.77)$ is between 0.90 and 0.95, and more exactly is 0.924. Hence
$$Pr(-1.77 \leqslant t) = 0.962.$$

7.6 By the method of Chapter 4,

	Q	Not Q	Total
Observed	220	765	985
Expected	246.25	738.75	985
O – E	– 26.25	26.25	

Hence

$$\chi^2 = (26.25 - 0.5)^2 \left(\frac{1}{246.25} + \frac{1}{738.75} \right) = 3.59.$$

This is less than 3.84, and the corresponding probability of the observed deviation being equalled or exceeded is greater than

0.05. More exactly (from other tables), the probability is 0.058. However, the original question relates to a number of Q-cells as few as or fewer than 220, and thus excludes from consideration an excess of Q-cells. The probability must therefore be halved, to give 0.029; the deficiency is statistically significant and again the null hypothesis that Q-cells occur with probability $\frac{1}{4}$ must be rejected. Check that had the χ^2 test been used in Exercise 4.13, it would have given $\chi^2 = 2.84$ and have led to a probability 0.046 (or 0.092/2); the numbers in Exercise 4.13 are too small for the χ^2 approximation to be trusted, but 0.046 is not very different from 0.037.

Calculations with y give

$$\sum y = 220$$
$$\sum y^2 = 220$$
$$\bar{y} = 220/985 = 0.2234$$
$$s^2 = (220 - 220^2/985)/984 = 0.1736$$
$$t = \frac{0.2234 - 0.2500}{\sqrt{(0.1736/985)}} = -2.00.$$

This t has so many d.f., 984, that it can be regarded as a Normal deviate; and the associated probability is slightly less than 0.05. Again the value must be halved because only a deficiency of Q-cells is under consideration, and hence the probability becomes slightly less than 0.25 (to compare with 0.29 by χ^2). The method is not as good as χ^2, but is of interest as illustrating the connections between different statistical techniques; refinements not presented here can bring the two into exact agreement. One advantage of this latest method is that, much as in Section 7.3, an upper limit for probability of a Q-cell can be calculated using the deviate 1.64 (from Table 7.1, final line) corresponding to a one-sided probability of 0.95, and assert that probability for Q is at most

$$0.2234 + 1.64\sqrt{(0.1736/985)} = 0.245.$$

Chapter 8

8.1

A	B	C		A	B	C
B	C	A	and	C	A	B
C	A	B		B	C	A

are only essentially distinct ways. From each, 5 more generated by substituting one of other orders of three letters for A, B, C so giving 12 squares in all. For example, order C, B, A means A replaced by C, B unaltered, C replaced by A, giving 2 new squares:

C	B	A		C	B	A
B	A	C	and	A	C	B
A	C	B		B	A	C

8.2

w	x	y	z
y	z	w	x
x	w	z	y
z	y	x	w

is only possibility except for replacing w, x, y, z by any other $23(= 4! - 1)$ orders such as y, x, z, w. Squares in Section 8.6 and new square are said to be *mutually orthogonal*.

8.3

Aα	Cβ	Eδ	Dε	Bγ
Dγ	Aε	Cα	Bδ	Eβ
Eε	Bα	Dβ	Cγ	Aδ
Bβ	Dδ	Aγ	Eα	Cε
Cδ	Eγ	Bε	Aβ	Dα

is one of at least 360 solutions.

8.4   First try inserting one Greek letter in north-west corner and 4 other places:

Aα	C	E	D	B
D	Eα	B	C	A
E	A	C	Bα	D
B	D	A	E	Cα
C	B	Dα	A	E

In second row, only permitted positions are with E, B, C. If we try E and proceed to row 3, rapidly find arrangement above is *only* possibility. Next try Bα instead of Eα in row 2; remaining rows cannot be completed. Same is true for Cα in row 2. Hence any Graeco-Latin square must be based on the structure already shown (α could be replaced by β, γ, δ, or ε without essential change.) Next try adding Cβ in Row 1. For Row 2, could have

$D\beta$ or $B\beta$ or $A\beta$, but none of these allows entering β according to rules on Rows 3, 4, 5. Cannot advance further and no Graeco-Latin square exists. This is standard way of discovering Graeco-Latin squares, but, with practice, one learns tricks to speed argument. Adequate catalogues of squares exist to help experimenters.

8.5 One of many solutions for 7 blocks of 3 is:

BCD, ACF, CEG, ABE, ADG, BFG, DEF.

Complementary blocks of 4 are:

AEFG, BDEG, ABDF, CDFG, BCEF, ACDE, ABCG.

8.6 For blocks in Exercise 8.5, one solution is:

D	G	E	A	F	C	B
F	A	G	B	C	E	D
C	B	F	D	E	A	G
G	C	A	F	B	D	E

8.7 Condition that each man has had each pub shows pattern of occupancy has been Latin square. Information given can be expressed:

	P	Q	R	S	T
1973	D				
1974	A			x	
1975	C	E	x	B	
1976	(E)		B	y	
1977	(B)		y		

Initially x and y are unknown, but we know same pub occurs in two positions; (E) is inserted because P must have had B or E in 1976 and R was occupying B. Now x must be D because A is already placed in 1974, and therefore in 1975 S had A. From row and column restrictions on two positions of y, this must be C. Can now easily reach.

D		A		
A		E		D
C	E	D	A	B
E	D	B	C	A
B		C		

and rest is trivial.

8.8   Write 16 letters in a 4×4 arrangement in any order:

$$
\begin{array}{cccc}
A & E & I & M \\
B & F & J & N \\
C & G & K & O \\
D & H & L & P
\end{array}
$$

Form sets of 4 from square finally obtained in Exercise 8.2, according to each of 5 categories in turn. Regard this as superposed on square finally obtained in Exercise 8.2. Then form 5 sets of 4 blocks of 4 using groupings according to columns (1–4), rows (5–8), large Roman letters (9–12), Greek (13–16) and small Roman (17–20):

1.	A	B	C	D		5.	A	E	I	M
2.	E	F	G	H		6.	B	F	J	N
3.	I	J	K	L		7.	C	G	K	O
4.	M	N	O	P		8.	D	H	L	P

9.	B	G	L	M		13.	D	G	I	N
10.	A	H	K	N		14.	C	H	J	M
11.	C	F	I	P		15.	A	F	L	O
12.	D	E	J	O		16.	B	E	K	P

17.	A	G	J	P
18.	C	E	L	N
19.	B	H	I	O
20.	D	F	K	M

8.9   See example in Section 8.8. If t different letters occur r times each, there are rt letters in all. These are arranged in sets of 3, so number of sets is $rt/3$, which must be an integer. Each set of 3 contributes 3 pairs, altogether $(rt/3) \times 3 = rt$ 'pairs of letters in same set'. Since $t(t-1)/2$ different pairs can be formed from t letters,

$$rt = pt(t-1)/2$$
$$\text{or } p = 2r/(t-1).$$

8.10 The design is closely related to those of Exercises 8.5 and 8.6. The merits have been discussed in Section 8.6, except for the additional control of position on stem which is analogous to a Latin square constraint.

Chapter 9

9.1 Using any method in solutions to Exercises 6.3 and 6.4, for each series separately,

$$\bar{y}_1 = 40.0, \qquad \bar{y}_2 = 35.0,$$
$$\sum (y - \bar{y}_1)^2 = 58.0, \quad \sum (y - \bar{y})^2 = 122.0$$

By Equation [9.X]

$$s^2 = \frac{58.0 + 122.0}{4 + 5} = 20.0 \text{ with 9 d.f.}$$

Then

$$\bar{y}_1 - \bar{y}_2 = 5.0,$$

$$Var(\bar{y}_1 - \bar{y}_2) = 20.0 \left(\frac{1}{5} + \frac{1}{6} \right) = 7.33 = (\text{approx.}) \ 2.71^2.$$

Limits are:

$$\mu_L = 5.0 - 2.71 \times 2.26 = -1.1,$$
$$\mu_U = 5.0 + 2.71 \times 2.26 = 11.1.$$

9.2 Means are same as in Exercise 9.1, but variability is much less:

$$s^2 = 42/9 = 4.67.$$

The limits now are 2.0, 8.0.

9.3 Limits at probability 0.95 are $-18.6, 28.6$. These three examples have exactly same values of $\bar{y}_1$ and $\bar{y}_2$, but differ widely in variability. Exercise 9.2 leaves no doubt that μ_1 is really greater than μ_2; Exercise 9.3 shows no appreciable evidence of difference; Exercise 9.1, despite no statistically significant difference, certainly hints that restriction of light may have real effect.

9.4 As rough approximation, one could say that s^2 will be about same, but $Var(\bar{y}_1 - \bar{y}_2)$ will contain factor $(1/10 + 1/12)$ instead of $(1/5 + 1/6)$. Hence $Var(\bar{y}_1 - \bar{y}_2)$ will be divided by 2. More exactly note that numerator s^2 is exactly doubled, but d.f. are now 20 instead of 9. Hence s^2 is reduced by a factor 9/10. SE of $(\bar{y}_1 - \bar{y}_2)$ is divided by approximately $\sqrt{2}$, more exactly by $\sqrt{(20/9)} = 1.49$. Table 7.1 shows that appropriate value of t is now 2.09 instead of 2.26. All changes combine to narrow range by a factor of about 1.6, so putting limits at 1.2, 8.8.

9.5 Method is outlined in Section 8.2. Values for y are formed by subtracting each deficient value from corresponding control, to give

Litter	y	y^2
I	1.4	1.96
II	0.9	0.81
III	1.1	1.21
IV	1.5	2.25
V	1.1	1.21
	6.0	7.44
		$7.20 = (6.0^2)/5$
		0.24

Hence $s^2 = \dfrac{0.24}{4} = 0.06$ with 4 d.f.

Mean advantage for control is $6.0/5 = 1.20$, with

$$SE = \sqrt{(0.06/5)} = \sqrt{0.012} = 0.11$$

Limits at probability 0.95 are

$$1.20 - 2.78 \times 0.11 = 0.89,$$
$$1.20 + 2.78 \times 0.11 = 1.51.$$

No serious doubt that deficient diet led to poorer weight gains; disadvantage estimated as 1.2 kg per animal and almost certainly between 0.9 kg and 1.5 kg per animal.

9.6 Total number of insects on the first 4 smooth plants must have been 4×48.5, and therefore mean of 5 plants is

$$(4 \times 48.5 + 110)/5 = 60.8.$$

Difference between rough and smooth is thus twice as great as was found for 9 plants, and entomologist naturally guesses that it will be more highly significant. However, occurrence of 110 in a group of 5 with other 4 averaging 48.5 suggests much greater variability than was previously found; increase in s^2 may be so great as to outweigh larger difference in numerator of t and increase in replication, so as to leave final value of t smaller than before.

Situation is unusual, but can occur. Statistician might inquire whether fifth smooth plant really was comparable with other 4, or whether perhaps it was mislaid at first because it was suspected to be different (e.g. already in flower and consequently more attractive to insects). Experiment is much too small for further discussion to be helpful, but it leaves suspicion that problem may have previously unsuspected complications.

Index